Sándor Szilassy

REVOLUTIONARY HUNGARY
1918-1921

Behind the Iron Curtain Series No. 9

Sándor Szilassy

REVOLUTIONARY HUNGARY

1918-1921

Published with the cooperation of the University of Tampa
by the Danubian Press, Inc. Astor Park, Florida, 32002.

International Standard Book Number: 0—87934—005—3
Library of Congress Catalog Card Number: 76—168832

Printed by: Sovereign Press

I PREFACE

Few countries had suffered more than Hungary during World War I. Hungary's losses in the first months of the war were numerically larger than all the other participants except Russia. Only the Serbs lost proportionately more men than Hungary did from 1914 to 1918.[1] The trenches at the front stank of blood and corpses; at home the population was starving, especially in the cities. The Wilsonian vision of a peaceful world conquered Hungary; at the same time the discontent of the nationalities shook the Dual Monarchy.

The events which transformed Europe from the armistice to the signing of the peace treaties are quite well known, but it is almost impossible to find a reliable description of the changes that took place in Hungary between 1918 and 1921. Accounts given by interested parties who were adherents either of the leftist liberal Károlyi regime, the communist Republic of Councils, or Admiral Horthy's counter-revolutionary, traditionalist governmental system are mostly biased. Moreover, the Hungarian language is unique and different. Most of the historical works on Hungary came to non-Magyar readers through foreign sources; essential Hungarian documents have been disregarded. It contributes to the difficulties that the political, social and economic fabric of the Magyar state developed for over a thousand years, but centuries-long dependence on the Habsburgs and Austria changed and distorted old concepts and made the realization of the age-old dream of complete independence impossible until 1918.

Many living persons were eyewitnesses of events which took place in the heated atmosphere of post World War I politics; some of them will probably disagree with certain conclusions. The author does not have first hand knowledge of events that he is writing about and regrets if he has done — unintentionally — injustice to people, parties or organizations in any way.

After more than 50 years, it is easy to say that Austrian and Hungarian statesmen should have avoided the war even at the price of great sacrifices. The Dualist system was a product of the acute crises of the Habsburg Empire which created many problems by solving others. It is true that it established a more or less stable governmental organization, provided protection against Russian and German expansionist policies, and secured the framework for industrial and agricultural development through economic autarchy. On the other hand, the peaceful decades of the rule of Francis Joseph were the seedbed where the nationalities grew richer and developed their intelligentsia, which increased old grievances and began to undermine the traditional political and social order.

It was also evident that the structure of the Habsburg Empire was loosening and a war — just or unjust — could only accelerate the process. Nineteen fourteen was the worst possible moment for a war — a world coalition turned against Germany and the Habsburg Monarchy. The Central Powers therefore had to take a much larger risk than their enemies did.[2] The dependence on Germany was steadily increasing during the war years. President Wilson's December 4, 1917 message to the Congress exaggerated the actual situation, but sang the song of the Hungarian extreme left too when it stated that "Austria-Hungary is for the time being not her own mistress, but simply the vassal of the German government. We must face the facts as they are and act upon them without sentiment in this stern business. The government of Austria-Hungary is not acting upon its own initiative or in response to the feelings of its own peoples, but as the instrument of another nation. We must meet its force with our own and regard the Central Powers as but one."[3] Since the purpose of the President was to "immediately declare the United States in a state of war with Austria-Hungary," the propaganda value of the statement was just as important as its concordance with the available evidence. On the other hand the President's statement also exonerated Hungary from war guilt, at least partly, by declaring her the instrument of another nation, thereby reinforcing the standpoint of the Hungarian leftist opposition about the necessity of separate peace and national independence.

The July 7, 1914 minutes of the Council of Ministers for Common Affairs prove that Hungarian Premier Count István Tisza had serious reservations about the wisdom of sending an ultimatum to the Serbs, who were almost in a hysterical state over the Austro-Hungarian annexation of Bosnia-Herzegovina. He believed that a surprise attack on Serbia was not advisable for moral and practical reasons: "Russia might be absorbed by Asian complications; Bulgaria, when it regains its strength, might want to revenge itself upon Serbia, which would all improve our position towards the problem of Greater Serbia, to what it is at present." Tisza wanted to wait, hoping that time would bring the solution without war. War Minister Krobatin remarked that the war between Russia and Japan, and also the Balkan war began without a foregoing declaration of war. It was the result of Tisza's suggestion to Francis Joseph that concrete demands were put up to Serbia first.

At the July 19 meeting of the Council of Ministers for Common Affairs it was Tisza again who foresaw the problem of war guilt. Upon his suggestion the government of the Monarchy declared that no war for conquest was intended and the annexation of the Kingdom of Serbia was not contemplated. Tisza's big mistake was that he did not protest publicly and finally acceded to issuing the ultimatum.

Sir Edward Grey, the British Foreign Minister never saw "one nation address to another a document of so formidable a character" than the ultimatum, although it was neither better nor worse than similar papers. In that era it was quite customary for great powers to interfere with the internal affairs of weaker countries from China to Turkey and moral indignation on the part of those who were tied by treaties to the Slavic cause was not justified. It turned out later that the murderers of Francis Ferdinand and his wife received their training in Serbia.

It should be added that the Central Powers won battles on many fronts in 1918. On March 3 in Brest-Litovsk the peace treaty with Soviet Russia was concluded; two days later the first draft of the peace treaty with Rumania was signed in Bucharest. Two enemy countries were knocked out of the war and in spring, 1918, the German offensive was rolling ahead in France. In the battle of Amiens which started on March 21, the Germans forced the British army units to retreat. At the end of May, the French troops were also driven back. Yet the considerably larger manpower and material resources of the Allies finally stopped the Central Powers on every front. On August 8, the German front in France collapsed at several points; on September 25 Bulgaria laid down her arms, and on the same day the hero of Liége, General Ludendorff himself, demanded that the German government should ask for an armistice on the basis of the 14 points of President Wilson. His request was granted on October 5th.

As a well known expert of Hungarian affairs noted, "submerged grievances rose suddenly and simultaneously to the surface. Among the Magyars of central Hungary a great wave of social unrest, largely borne of war-weariness, swept over the dispossessed classes. Simultaneously, the long-repressed Magyar nationalism broke into revolt against the Habsburg connection, feeling obscurely, and certainly with no more than partial justice, that it was through that connection that Hungary had been dragged into the war."[4]

At the end of the war, Count Mihály Károlyi emerged as the only political leader in Hungary who could stand on the basis of "I said so..." His humanistic, pro-Western platform did not prove to be practical for the newly independent country in an era of nationalistic and chauvinistic aspirations.

The communist leadership which grabbed the power from Károlyi consisted of doctrinaires. They misjudged the internal and external situation and after initial victories over the invaders had to yield to foreign pressure and resign. The Trade

Union Government of Gyula Peidl was overthrown by a coup d'etat, but the royalist regime of Joseph Habsburg was not tolerated by the Allies and finally Admiral Horthy took over.

The sessions of the National Assembly, the tragedy of the Trianon peace treaty, the romantic attempts of Charles IV to regain the throne in 1921, and the efforts for political and economic consolidation are parts of the kaleidoscopic story which is unfolded on the following pages.

It contains important elements of modern political and social history. Many new concepts were introduced first in Hungary which paid for them so dearly with human and physical resources during the revolutionary era. At the end of World War I Europe was shifting from old forms of political and social order to others; Hungary became a testing ground. Károlyi kept some of the old rules; he asked the King to relieve him and his government of their oath before the People's Republic was proclaimed. When Kun, Friedrich and Horthy took over they did not worry too much about formalities.

International diplomacy was again transformed into a confusing power game in Paris. The Italians were disappointed,[5] Americans discouraged, and many British politicians were unhappy about the French domination of continental affairs. Hungary lost most of her territory and population and became the militarily and economically weak pauper of Central Europe. Dreams of past glory and irredenta became the guiding elements of her policy for the next two decades.

II. THE BEGINNING OF THE END

World War I practically ended for Hungary when the armistice between the Allied and Associated Powers and Austria-Hungary was concluded in Padua on November 3rd, 1918, under the severest conditions, as the result of the victorious Italian advancement. Military authorities completely misinterpreted the actual situation before the collapse, which contributed to the general confusion. Prince Schönburg, commander of the Austro-Hungarian 6th Army, reported on October 22, 1918, that "the Piave front is strong," and that he was not worried about a serious enemy attack.[6] Shortly after this, on October 30th, the daily report of Fieldmarshal von Borovic confessed the withdrawal of the 6th army to the "früher erwaehnte Linie;" in reality this meant the troops were streaming in disorder toward the hinterland.

The military clauses of the armistice stipulated the complete demobilization of the Austro-Hungarian army, and Allied occupation of "any strategic points of Austria-Hungary, deemed by these Powers necessary in order to render any military operations possible or to maintain order."[7] One of the obvious deficiencies of the armistice was its scope. It settled the war between Italy and the Monarchy, but left open the fate of Hungary, which was represented at the armistice negotiations only by a low-ranking officer.[8]

The process of dissolution had run its course by that time. The war had consumed the economic strength of the country. Capital resources had dwindled to a fraction of pre-war value; agricultural and non-military industrial production had decreased dangerously. Revolutionary sentiment characterized the workers' movement as well as the armed forces in Budapest and in the countryside. Military leaders blamed the agitation of former prisoners-of-war who were sent back home from Russia.[9] According to Minister of Defense Szurmay, "a committee was organized in America, which was supposed to send people to Germany, for the purpose of the organization of powerful destructive propaganda."[10] Other memoranda of the Defense Ministry reported newly established anti-Monarchy revolutionary newspapers, networks from Omsk to Paris, and mutinies in the Austro-Hungarian army during which the officers did not intervene but stayed in their apartments or left the scene of riots.[11]

Anti-government organizations endangered the war effort from the beginning. Austrian and Hungarian Social De-

In 1910 Jews numbered 909,000 or 5 per cent of the total population. They were not considered a nationality, but members of an officially recognized ("received") church from 1894.

Magyarization was, of course, the inevitable consequence of opportunism, compulsory education, Hungarian supremacy, and urbanization. In 1910 about 80 per cent of the urban population was Hungarian; industrialization and the growth of the cities made them a melting pot for non-Hungarians. Still, the masses of Slavs and other nationalities — especially on the fringe areas of the country — created a delicate situation for the Budapest government.

It should be remarked that the Hungarian handling of the nationality question was probably influenced by the policy of the Imperial Government, which during the Revolution of 1848-49 stirred up nationalities in Hungary and used them against the revolutionary army in its fight for liberal-democratic reforms and independence. Wounds heal slowly, and historical injuries upset the balance of the national thinking.

The unsolved question of the franchise also contributed to the difficulties in Hungary. There was no comprehensive electoral reform since 1848. An extension of the voting rights and even universal suffrage was annually discussed in the Budapest Parliament, but a democratic electoral law never had been accepted. Even Francis Joseph himself had been unable to force it through in 1905, when the minority government of Baron Géza Fejérváry became an obedient tool of the royal will. Because of the electoral restrictions the Hungarian Parliament was the only one in Europe in which there was no Socialist deputy. In 1914, only 8% of the population had voting rights.

The shrinking of the old gentry created a special problem in Hungary. Unlike the wealthy land owners, the common nobility in many cases lost their titles as well as landholdings following the liberation of the serfs in 1848 and were forced to accept government positions. Instead of the patriotic and formerly independent farmers, the small but powerful group of the rich "magnates" took over leading positions in politics and in the fast developing capitalist economy. They were dependent on the Habsburg rule by tradition as well as interest. Because of their influence in Vienna it was easy for them to form a political mafia, which ruled Hungary for decades after the Compromise of 1867. Counts and Princes from the Andrássy, Batthyány, Károlyi, Khuen-Héderváry, Szapáry, Serényi, Pálffy, Pallavicini, Esterházy, Windischgraetz and other aristocratic families became Ministers and Prime Ministers in a number of Hungarian governments. The composition of the governments frequently was decided upon in the National Casino, the exclusive club of the higher nobility and its adherents. The theoretical equality of the House of Magnates and the Lower House increased the influence of the aristocracy. Elected representatives had to compete with members of the high nobility whenever an important piece of legislation had to be approved by the ruler. Frequently the magnates won, and the people lost.

The Heir Apparent, Archduke Francis Ferdinand, whose murder started the war, saw the perils and proposed reforms which would have transformed his country into a federal state. In spite of his serious lung ailment he worked very diligently on plans which would have guaranteed equal cultural and political rights to all peoples comprising the Austro-Hungarian Monarchy. But even he could not do much against the resistance of the traditional forces which stood on the basis of the Compromise of 1867. The plans of the Archduke were especially unpopular in Hungary, because they were directed against the territorial integrity of the country.

The trade balance of the Monarchy was positive between 1886 and 1906; later, it always closed with a loss. In 1907 the deficit was 45 million crowns; in 1912 it increased to 823 million. Financial experts tried to fill the gap with foreign loans, but they were unable to heal the disease caused by excessive armament and constant military preparedness as well as outdated production methods. Consequently there was a decrease of exports and an increase of imports.

After a long, comparatively peaceful period, many Euro-

14

peans were excited about the possibility of adventures and did not believe that "war is a very crude and poor substitute for reason and morality. Like revolution, it can solve problems only in an incomplete and summary way, arousing new difficulties, new injustices," as Oszkár Jászi, a liberal Hungarian theoretician, wrote.

Economic inequality and historical grievances added to the problems. As the Serb Minister President, Pasic, told a visitor, the national and economic progress of his country were closely related. "Only by placing our agricultural products advantageously in the world-market shall we be able to obtain the funds needed for an industrial expansion. At present [in 1912] we are totally cut off from the world-market. Hence the purchases we must make abroad are costly and we cannot turn to account the produce of our soil. The custom barriers of Austria-Hungary stand at our frontiers."

"What we need is a trade treaty with the most-favored nation treatment, a free port at any suitable Adriatic harbor, and commonly agreed transit traffic charges. Given those things, we could become trustworthy neighbors instead of irreconcilable enemies, eventually even allies of your powerful Monarchy."

"The animosity felt throughout my land for the Monarchy derives directly from the stranglehold of duties Hungary puts on us. Our farmer fattens his pigs for nothing, our townsman has to pay an absurd price for every shirtbutton and scrap of cloth he wears because in our hopeless economic plight we can neither develop our industry nor exploit the fruits of our soil."

"I am a man of peace, but Austria-Hungary pushes me on the road to war."[13]

Of course, the peace views of Pasic were not entirely shared by the Serbian press and the secret societies which were partially controlled by the government. The organs of *emigré* Serb groups frequently wrote more openly about the aims of Serbia than the Belgrade press could. The December 3, 1913 issue of the Chicago journal *Srbobran* called for murder: "The Austrian Heir Apparent has announced his intention of visiting Sarajevo early next year. Every Serb will take note of this. Serbs, seize everything you can lay hand on — knives, rifles, bombs and dynamite. Take holy vengeance! Death to the Habsburg dynasty, eternal remembrance to the heroes who raise their hands against it."

It is evident that although the war began against the Serbs, it also turned the Slavs of the Habsburg Empire against the ruling house. The Czechs, the Poles and the South-Slavs, in alliance with the Rumanians of Transylvania, represented a sizeable proportion of the Monarchy's population.

Emperor Wilhelm of Germany and his government did not make a secret of their contempt for Austria-Hungary. During a conversation with Prince Lajos Windischgraetz in the early part of the war Wilhelm remarked that in view of Francis Joseph's advanced age and the indubitable fact that after the cessation of hostilities Germany would dominate Europe economically as well as politically, the merger of the Austro-Hungarian Empire with his own country was inevitable. Bethmann-Hollweg, the Chancellor of Germany instructed the Ministry of Foreign Affairs on September 7, 1914: "It is urgently desirable that the Hungarian government guarantee concessions to the Rumanians," in other words to cede Transylvania to Rumania in return for joining the Central Powers. It is evident that a German victory also could have destroyed the Monarchy.

At the end of the war, open rebellions broke out in every nook of the country; at the front Czech artillerymen frequently shot at German, Austrian and Hungarian troops from behind; sabotage disrupted the production of war materials.

Internal dissent, military defeats and general impoverishment all contributed to the crisis of the monarchy, but the main force behind it was the rising tide of nationalism. Austria, which had more Slavs than Germans, could not maintain her orientation toward Germany without Hungarian assistance. In 1918 she lost both the internal and external support.

16

III. THE COLLAPSE

On June 20th, 1918, Prime Minister Wekerle dealt in the Hungarian parliament with the intervention of the gendarmerie in the machine-factory of the State Railroads, which ended with "death and many injuries," and stated that the evidence available to him proved that "it was an organized workers' movement, which unfortunately extended to the whole capitol city, and even further."[14] Discontent was growing in every area.

In 1918, the entire continent of Europe was burning with the passion for ending the bloody war, and the desire for peace was nowhere stronger than in Budapest. James W. Gerard, the American ambassador to Germany, reported as early as January 16th, 1917, that high government circles in the Hungarian capitol city were eager to establish peace with the Allies.[15] Frederic C. Penfield, the American diplomatic representative in Vienna, explained to Secretary of State Lansing in his report of September 16th, 1917, that in Austria there was no press freedom or freedom of expression in general, but in Hungary the real situation was presented to the public by parliamentary debates and the press had not been muted.[16]

It is a fact that Count Gyula Andrássy, before accepting the position of Foreign Minister, made preliminary investigations in Switzerland for Charles IV about the possibilities for the liquidation of the war, which could not be won after the withdrawal of the German troops. Andrássy returned from Switzerland with the impression that the future of the Monarchy was not hopeless, and that England and France were willing to help to save it. For this reason, the Czechs and Serbs intended to create a military and political situation which could not be changed easily.

The Rumanians were especially eager to avenge the military defeat and unite with their brothers. Diplomacy and propaganda were both used to accomplish this goal. Two weeks after America's entry into the war, on April 18, 1917, a

17

Rumanian delegation headed by Vasile Lucacius left for Washington. During their trip through Russia, they stopped at the Darnitza prisoner-of-war camp and asked the leaders of the Rumanian captives to issue a proclamation in which they demanded the unification of Transylvania with their occupied homeland. The declaration was printed later in American newspapers, copies of which were dropped by American airplanes over the trenches of the Austro-Hungarian army. The members of the delegation organized mass meetings in Washington, Cleveland, New York and other cities, issued the bilingual periodical *Romania,* and cooperated with Masaryk, Paderewski, Hinkovici and Zhotkowich, who represented Czech, Polish, South Slav and Ruthenian organizations in the United States. The Rumanian campaign was successful. Following the cabinet meeting of November 4, 1918, Secretary of State Lansing issued a declaration promising support for just Rumanian political and territorial rights at the Peace Conference.

President Wilson promised "the freest opportunity of autonomous development" to the peoples of Austria-Hungary in the tenth of his Fourteen Points, not the dissolution of the monarchy, but the Central European situation was changing fast. The State Department felt that it had to adjust its policies according to French and British interests in order to finish the war as quickly as possible.

A National Committee of Rumanian Unity was formed in Paris on October 3, under the chairmanship of Take Jonescu. Similar organizations were set up in England and Italy. The Unity Committee was officially recognized by the Allied governments during the period of October 12—November 22, and Rumanian aspirations got the backing of the leading Entente powers.

The internal conditions in the Austro-Hungarian empire were turning from bad to worse. The governments in Vienna as well as in Budapest were powerless before the demands of the nationalities; the remaining reliable troops were tied down at the front. The Poles proclaimed their independence in Warsaw on October 7th; the Czech government was formed in Paris on October 14th; on October 15th Croatia declared her independence in Zagreb, and on October 16th Emperor-King Charles issued a Manifesto in which he authorized the transformation of the monarchy into a federal state. (The integrity of the possessions of the Hungarian Crown were theoretically not affected by it. The Hungarian Premier threatened Austria with the stoppage of food supplies if Hungary's frontiers were not guaranteed.)

Emperor Charles made a last attempt for separate peace by sending Prince Lajos Windischgraetz to Switzerland. He negotiated with the diplomatic representatives of France, Great Britain and the United States. Five days later a French note was handed to Windischgraetz:

The Government of the Republic of France finds it necessary to inform the representatives of His Imperial and Royal Apostolic Majesty as follows: In view of the fact that the peoples of the hitherto Austro-Hungarian Monarchy have resolved on the dissolution of the Danubian State, the Government of the Republic of France regards itself as being in no position to continue negotiations with the Government of His Imperial and Royal Apostolic Majesty. In consequence thereof the talks so far pursued must be considered as null and void of application.

The text of the British and American notes was identical. President Wilson stated on October 21 that he could no longer accept autonomy as a precondition of peace. The dissolution of the Monarchy was going on. The Allies were unwilling to save it, although the Hungarian Social Democratic party had a platform which at that time seemed to be acceptable to every shade of the political spectrum, except to the arch-conservatives. The October 8 Manifesto of the party summarized the demands of the democratic left in ten points:

1. A new government must be formed at once from the representatives of the democratic classes and of all nations [nationalities] of the country.

2. The government should dissolve Parliament and proceed with the election of a Constituent Assembly on the basis of universal suffrage, to be extended to women also.
3. It should offer the enemy states immediate peace according to the ideas of the Russian proletarian revolution and [President] Wilson.
4. It should make an end to national oppression.
5. It should democratize [public] administration and guarantee the right to association, assembly and union organization.
6. It should give the land to those who cultivate it.
7. It should socialize the factories which have outgrown individual control.
8. By a just policy of taxation, it should transfer the burden of the war costs to the owners of large estates.
9. It should initiate labor legislation, start broad measures for social welfare, and make preparations for the introduction of the eight-hour workday.
10. It should take care of those who are returning from the war fronts and compensate the disabled, the war widows and orphans.[17]

A Hungarian National Council was formed in Budapest on October 25th under the leadership of Count Mihály Károlyi, with the aims of separate peace, national independence and democratic reforms. Military censorship was terminated on the previous day; therefore, the proclamation of the Council could be published without difficulties. The first four points demanded the removal of the "corrupt parliamentary and governmental system," independence in the military, economic and diplomatic fields, and immediate armistice or peace. The fifth point was aimed at the solution of the nationality problem:

The right of self-determination must be secured for the non-Magyar speaking peoples of our country without hesitation, according to the Wilsonian principles, hoping that these principles do not endanger the territorial integrity of Hungary, but place it on a most secure basis.

The cultural and local autonomy of the nationalities should be as broad as possible, because the peaceful competition of different cultures can only benefit the material, intellectual and moral development of the peoples of the country. In such a Hungary, the poisonous problems that existed between the nation and the nationalities would be meaningless. The country would be transformed into a fraternal alliance of equal peoples.

The National Council did not have any authority; therefore, the impatient population wanted to occupy the palace of Archduke Joseph, the King's plenipotentiary, to force the nomination of Count Károlyi to Prime Minister. At the Suspension Bridge, mounted police drove back the demonstrators, and from the rear other policemen opened fire, killing and wounding several people. This incident turned Budapest over to Károlyi. Police officers, railway employees, factory workers, manufacturers and the army expressed their solidarity with the Council. The soldiers no longer obeyed the orders of General Lukachich, commander of the local garrison.

After the incident Károlyi decided to send his lovely and energetic wife to see her stepfather, Foreign Minister Count Andrássy in Vienna, to describe the gravity of the situation to him and to ask him to recommend to Charles "the only thing to be done: to recognize the National Council and at once to appoint the new Government in accordance with its desire," as Károlyi wrote in his *Memoirs.* "I knew that he was always ready to believe things to be as he would like them to be. I suspected that he would read the newspaper reports from Budapest with skepticism, would discount them as merely the tales of journalists in sympathy with us, and would persuade himself that the true facts of the situation were very different." When Countess Károlyi had a moment alone with Andrássy she told him how things were going in Budapest. Seeing his daughter's anxiety Andrássy's eyes filled with tears. She emphasized that the public didn't have confidence in anyone but Károlyi, and the appointment of somebody else would throw the country into the arms of Bolshevism.

The news saddened Andrássy, but he attached no great importance to the turn of events in Budapest. He complained instead of the problems he had in Vienna. "On the 29th, he said, there had actually been a demonstration against him. Three Prussian officers were said to be skulking in the neighborhood, with the object of carrying him off in a motor. The Czechs, too, were completely drunk. They had made that fool Masaryk President of their Republic!"

His efforts in Vienna failing, Károlyi issued another proclamation to the army on October 30th, referring to the example of the Croatian and Czech troops who had recognized the authority of their National Councils earlier. The proclamation stated that "Hungarian troops were not ordered to the frontiers of the country to guard Hungary's integrity until the peace treaty would be signed, but were ordered to Budapest to dissolve the National Council which wants immediate peace, complete independence, national army, Hungarian Foreign Ministry, people's rule and social justice for the working and suffering masses, for poor men everywhere." It emphasized that the Council wanted neither bloodshed nor disorder, asked the soldiers not to shoot at their brothers and mothers, then continued: "The Hungarian National Council stands on the basis of national self-determination ... Hungarian soldiers, don't be the hangmen of freedom and prison guards of independence. The Hungarian people want to cooperate with all other nations in a brotherly way, respecting the principle of the mutual recognition of liberty and national independence."

On the afternoon of the 30th, most military establishments in Budapest were taken over by mutinous soldiers. On the morning of the 31st, the telephone rang in the Astoria Hotel at Károlyi's headquarters. Designated Prime Minister Hadik wanted to see him. Together they went to the palace of the Archduke, where Hadik submitted his resignation. Joseph immediately appointed Károlyi Prime Minister in Charles' name.

After the publication of the news, Budapest was bubbling over with exuberance. Open trucks carried soldiers and civilians through the streets; mums decorated caps, buttonholes and rifles. The revolution that was supposed to convert Hungary into an independent, democratic country had begun peacefully.

IV. THE PEOPLE'S REPUBLIC

Károlyi was finally in the saddle. His government consisted of representatives of the left wing of the Independence Party, the Radical Bourgeois Party, and the Social Democratic Party. None of these parties had any experience in the transaction of governmental affairs, except on the negative side. They were always in the opposition, arguing and fighting with each other as well as with the representatives of the administration. Their ideas were different in regard to the future course of Hungary as well as to the internal reorganization of the government and its agencies. All they agreed upon was complete independence and the deposal of the House of Habsburg, hoping that radical constitutional changes would greatly contribute to the solution of other problems. The chaotic situation resulted in fighting between Hungarian and Bosnian troops in Budapest, the freeing of a man by the mob who attempted to kill former Prime Minister Tisza, and proposals that Count Gyula Andrássy and others should be banished from the country. One of the first decrees issued by the new government was the prohibiting of all freight traffic toward Germany and Austria on the Danube river, which hurt Hungarian interests, broke international commitments, and did not turn Allied sympathies toward Hungary either.

On November 1st, one day after the government was sworn in, the National Council demanded the transformation of Hungary into a republic. The disintegration of the Monarchy continued; the conclusion had to be drawn.[18] Joseph telephoned the King repeatedly, asked him not to block the way of the peoples' will, and emphasized that the monarchy was lost forever in Hungary.[19] Finally Charles relieved Károlyi of his oath and on November 13th "renounced participation in the affairs of the state," declaring that he recognized in advance whatever decision Hungary might take regarding its future form of state. On the 16th, the National Council dissolved parliament and proclaimed a People's Republic with Károlyi as provisional President. On January 11th, 1919, the appointment was made definitive.

Károlyi was a controversial man whose ambition, vanity and lust for power can be traced back to some of his childhood experiences. He was born with harelips and in spite of the wealth and power of his family frequently was the object of mockery and unjust humiliation on the part of his playmates. Once already as a boy he shouted: "Wait, just wait, the day will come when you will see who Mihály Károlyi is!" He played the role of a playboy for years, lost and won fortunes at the card table, drank in bars and organized gay parties which were the talk of Budapest. Later young Károlyi cooled down, studied agronomy, sociology and politics, and at the age of thirty he was a new man. Constant practicing largely eliminated his speech defect and at the outbreak of the war Károlyi was a well known although unpopular speaker in the Hungarian parliament.

The new chief of the Hungarian state changed his political convictions quite often before the war. At the beginning of his political career, he was a faithful follower of conservative Prime Minister Count István Tisza, but — before the start of World War I — he was accused by his opponents of initiating secret negotiations with the French, with the objective of pulling Hungary away from Germany. At the outbreak of the war, he was returning from the United States to Europe, and spent several months in a French concentration camp. According to contemporary rumors (which he denied), he was released only when he promised that he would do everything he could for the quick termination of the fighting.

The conversion of Károlyi from his traditionalistic and con-

24

servative views to the tactics of violence and republicianism which he preached in Budapest and all over the country in the second half of the war was having deep effects, because basically he was an honest man whose personal interests were contrary to the new developments. He was one of the wealthiest men in the entire Monarchy. His ancestor, General Sándor Károlyi, surrendered to the Habsburg army in 1711; as a result of this he received peerage and huge land holdings which were confiscated from rebel supporters of Ferenc Rákóczi.

As a man of action, Count Károlyi needed advisers. He could have chosen some of the best brains in the country, but preferred to rely on the advice of politically inexperienced newspapermen and other adherents of the extreme left. His connections with the Social Democratic Party were especially warm.

Károlyi was openly pacifist and pro-Entente in 1917. He said in a speech in January of that year, that "in the future ... those will be considered cultured nations which put away selfish aims, find the way of general disarmament and have the strength and courage to fight for peace."[20]

In another speech that he delivered in the city of Cegléd on September 17th, Károlyi announced that he would participate at a peace meeting in Switzerland. In that country he said in an interview that he was seeking connections with British and American representatives. Oszkár Jászi, a liberal intellectual arranged a meeting between Károlyi and Middleton Edwards, the British Consul in Geneva who convinced the Hungarians that America's intervention in the war was not the "mere bluff" which the press offices of the Central Powers called it, but a "terrible reality" of which it was hardly possible for Europeans to perceive the full dimensions and importance.[21]

The Budapest daily *Az Ujság* learned that Károlyi also negotiated with J. Caillaux, a member of the French parliament, about separate peace. Caillaux' parliamentary immunity was waived in December, and he was sentenced to prison because of his dealings with the enemy. Károlyi was not harmed. At that time, King Charles was also involved in separate peace negotiations which were conducted by Prince Sixtus, his Belgian brother-in-law.

Hungary's international position was not as grave as it looked when the leftist-liberal Károlyi regime took over. Count Revertera, the special emissary of Foreign Minister Count Andrássy in Switzerland, reported in a telegram sent through the Bern embassy of the monarchy on October 31st, that Professor de Münnynck, a trusted friend of Clemenceau and Foch, was waiting in Freiburg for an Austrian or Hungarian diplomat who had to be authorized to discuss the following peace program: "1. The establishment of the maximum territorial losses that Austria-Hungary can endure, without its collapse. It must be emphasized that authoritative French circles do not wish to cede Triest or a large area to Italy. 2. The maximum should be determined as such that Austria-Hungary can grant in view of her internal political situation, without causing the disintegration of the country. 3. The economic life of Austria-Hungary should not be endangered."

De Vaux, the ambassador of the monarchy in Bern, added to this that "the representative of Clemenceau and Foch will be accompanied by an Englishman. These gentlemen will act in an official capacity, which makes possible the discussion of the basic issues of a separate peace."[22]

The influential *Frankfurter Zeitung* published a report from London on October 29th, which stated that British government circles were willing to negotiate with Andrássy only, but it was evident that the preservation of the monarchy was not made dependent on personalities, and Károlyi's envoys were just as welcome as Andrássy's would have been. Anyhow, there was almost no difference between Károlyi and Andrássy in the evaluation of the situation. As soon as he occupied the position of Foreign Minister, Count Andrássy notified Kaiser Wilhelm of Germany through Emperor-King Charles, that the Monarchy was unable to continue the struggle and would ask for a separate peace, in order to avoid its collapse.

Károlyi did not use the opportunity that presented itself on the day when he took office, although he must have learned about it from Andrássy, who was his father-in-law.[23] The new Hungarian Minister to Switzerland was Róza Bédi-Schwimmer, a feminist leader. She did not contact the emissary of the French leaders, made several other mistakes (one of them was the quoting of a secret, coded telegram in open form), and finally an old diplomat, Baron Gyula Szilassy, had to take over the legation.[24]

It seemed that the territorial integrity of the country still could be saved by conciliatory gestures toward the nationalities. Jászi, the Minister of Nationality Affairs, wanted to transform Hungary into an "eastern Switzerland" considering as a model the concept of Lajos Kossuth, whose principal aims were "reconciliation of national discord, security against external aggression, absorption by and dependence upon a suprapower by joint armed forces, and the establishment of a customs union."

It was too late for reconciliation between Magyars and the nationalities, as it turned out. The undeniable honesty and sincerity of Jászi and Károlyi were not considered satisfactory guarantees for the leaders of the Slavs and Rumanians, whose goals at that time far exceeded limited sovereignty.

The five-month rule of the Károlyi regime did not solve other burning problems of Hungary either. There was unemployment in the factories and starvation in the cities. In contrast to a 300-1000 per cent increase in the prices of consumer goods, the workers' wages were raised only by 100-120 per cent. In peace time, a worker could buy one kilogram (more than two pounds) of meat from one hour's wage; in the first months of 1919, he had to work 10 to 12 hours for it. The proportion of prices and wages was similar in regard to other consumer goods.[25]

The promised land reform did not materialize. Károlyi distributed a part of his vast holdings among the peasants, but the rest of the aristocracy did not follow his example. Elections were promised, but not held. Extremist agitation

27

increased, and the defenseless country was attacked from the north, east, and south by Slavs and Rumanians.²⁶ Members of the Károlyi government took pacifism seriously. Béla Linder, Minister of Defense, "never again wanted to see a soldier" according to his November 1st address to the assembled troops. The Social Democratic party was dominant in the coalition government; Linder was not in a position to stop the propaganda of the socialist emissaries at railroad stations and military barracks, even if he wanted to. Revolutionary indoctrination and disarming was the goal, but the soldiers were quite unwilling to return to their homes and start working again, in spite of the lack of manpower — especially in farming areas. The Socialists were anti-militaristic by ideology as well as practical considerations. They were afraid that an overwhelmingly peasant army would be unreliable and eventually wanted to organize an elite workers' army, but their role in the coalition government was simply negative in regard to national defense. A proposal according to which fourteen acres of land would be given to those who voluntarily joined the revolutionary army and served at least two years was voted down.

The right of self-determination and plebiscites which were supposed to be the basic pillars of Wilsonian principles and in which the new Hungarian regime placed its trust, were quickly forgotten by the victorious Allies. In connection with Hungarian complaints about the steady advance of Rumanian troops in Hungarian territory, the Allied High Command explained on December 18 that "the Entente regarded Rumania as an Allied Power, whose army had the same right as those of the other Allied Powers to take part in the occupation of the areas defined in the Armistice agreement." It was evident that crude force and not majestic ideas decided Hungary's fate. Still, Károlyi hoped that his democratic policy would provide a satisfactory solution for the nationalities. The Minister of Nationality Affairs, Oszkár Jászi, who opened up negotiations with their representatives in Nevember, offering them complete autonomy and a federative political system, knew that it was too late. Most of them turned their backs on Hungary.

Károlyi initiated separate peace negotiations with the French and emphasized in Belgrade before General Franchet d'Esperay on November 7th, 1918, that his regime was not responsible for the acts of past political leaders, wanted to achieve democracy, give voting rights to all citizens, and distribute the land among those who tilled it. When he mentioned President Wilson and his democratic pacifist principles, "the General waved his hand contemptuously."[27]

The new armistice agreement was signed between the Allies and Hungary on November 13th. It forced President Károlyi to withdraw his shrinking army north of the line traced by the upper valley of the Szamos and Besztercze rivers, and west of the river Maros to its union with the Tisza. In the South the armistice line was drawn beyond the cities of Szabadka, Baja and Pécs "in such a manner that these places remain unoccupied by the Hungarian troops," in other words they were given to the Serbs.[28]

The demobilization of the Hungarian military and naval forces (with the exception of six infantry and two cavalry divisions destined for the maintenance of public order) and the right of the Allies to occupy all places and points of strategic significance were among the stipulations. Post offices, telephone and telegraph lines, and the railway service were placed under the control of the Entente. Mackensen's German units, which were heading back to Germany from Rumania through Hungarian territory, were ordered to get out within fifteen days. After all these, the 17th point assured Károlyi that "the Allies will not interfere with the internal administration of the Hungarian State." This statement was somewhat illusory.

On November 13th, the day on which the armistice was signed, news arrived to Budapest about the appearance of Czech troops in North Hungary. Dr. Stodola, the envoy of the Prague government in Hungary, explained that those were irregulars and that they would be withdrawn. He asked the Hungarian authorities to be patient and not to shoot at the regular troops that would force the guerillas out from Hungary.[29] Of course, both the regulars and the irregulars continued their advance. Stodola's diversionary tactics made it possible for them to occupy additional territories without resistance.

Károlyi complained to the Peace Conference, but didn't get any assistance. Only the Italians gave some cautious support to Hungary, but it was more anti-Yugoslav than pro-Hungarian.

In early January, 1919, an American political mission, headed by Archibald C. Coolidge, a history professor, arrived in Vienna to study the quickly changing Central European situation. After spending some days in Vienna, Coolidge traveled to Budapest where he was warmly received.

His report of January 19th to the American Peace Commission referred to Hungarian informants and stated that "Hungary forms a natural geographic and economic unity to a greater extent than any other state in Europe except Great Britain." The river system, food producing and industrial areas that supplemented each other, were all supporting the idea that Hungary needed a treatment as a whole, in Coolidge's opinion.

This was one of the few friendly gestures of the Allies toward the Károlyi government. Colonels Miles and Causey examined the problem of the new national boundaries, but were chased away by the Serbs and did not accomplish anything constructive.[30] Democratic Hungary was not invited to Paris, but representatives of the surrounding states had many opportunities to outline their territorial aims.

E. Benes, the Czechoslovak emissary, stated on February 19th, 1919, before the Supreme Council that — with the help of the Allies — he and his associates organized three armies who fought not for territory, but only for "the principles of the United Nations." His oratory against "a medieval Dynasty backed by bureaucracy, militarism, the Roman Catholic church, and, to some extent, by high finance" could have been as popular in Hungary as it probably was in Prague, but Hungarians did not set up organizations in the Allied countries during the war to gain sympathy for the country's independence and official recognition for the national aspirations. It is also true that Károlyi rose to political power too late to do so.

He could not curb or balance the Communist propaganda spread by the Vörös Ujság (Red News), the organ of the Communist Party of Hungary which was founded on November 24, 1918 by Béla Kun and his collaborators. The tone of agitation was so sharp that Lenin himself sent a rebuttal to his Hungarian comrades. Kun told him in his reply: "Please be assured ... I will handle things in a firm Marxist manner. No coup d'etat of any kind will be possible until we will be ready to take the power in our hands."

When four policemen were killed as a result of a demonstration at the editorial offices of the newspaper of the Social Democratic party, Kun and others were imprisoned but emerged as heroes from prison after the liberal press reported that they were badly beaten by the police.[31] Even the transcripts of police examinations were printed. The number of followers of this earlier insignificant party increased. Opportunists also joined its ranks.

Hungary was in a desperate position when Lieutenant Colonel Vyx, the plenipotentiary of the Paris Peace Conference in Hungary, demanded the evacuation of a large part of Central Hungary for the invading Rumanians on March 20th, 1919. "Disorder, anarchy, counter-revolutionary diversion reached their peak then," according to Böhm, the Minister of Defense. Vyx threw a flaming torch into the gasoline barrel by the note of the Peace Conference which he gave to Károlyi in the presence of Prime Minister Berinkey and the Minister of Defense.

He declared that the Hungarian troops had to be withdrawn behind the new armistice line, which represented the provisional political boundary of the country The ultimatum stretched out the Rumanian-occupied area 50 to 80 kilometers

31

to the west, and gave the Hungarians only 24 hours during which the troop withdrawal had to begin. The sudden urgency could not be easily explained, because the Allied note was drafted at the February 26th meeting of the Peace Conference, almost one month before it was delivered.

Vyx told Károlyi that the note was final, and it had to be accepted in full without reservations on March 21st before 6 p.m. He declared that in the case of a negative answer the Allied missions would leave Budapest immediately. This could have meant the end of the armistice and the resumption of war with the victorious Entente.

The Hungarian President made it clear that the demands of the Allies were unjustified, because the new demarcation line would mean the enemy occupation of areas with Hungarian population, would be contrary to the Belgrade armistice, would take away from Hungary areas that belonged to the country for several centuries, and would make economic reconstruction impossible.

According to an article that Károlyi published in the July 25th, 1919 issue of the Social Democratic *Arbeiter Zeitung* in Vienna, he called together the Council of Ministers after returning from Vyx and declared that the coalition government could not be maintained, because the bourgeois parties lost their popular support, and only a Social Democratic regime would be in a position to maintain public order. "If we don't want to fulfill the murderous demands of the Entente, we must have a unified army. In this period of economic depression and strengthening class struggle [communist demonstrations and trouble making were the order of the day], only the Social Democratic Party could organize an army of unity. Western orientation and policies built on Wilsonian principles are definitely over. We need a new orientation which would secure for us the sympathy of the [Socialist] International of the workers."

Károlyi was convinced that a socialist government would have the support of the bourgeoise and could sign an agreement with the Communists which would insure internal peace for the duration of the life-death struggle with the invaders.

According to the unanimous resolutions of the Council of Ministers, the government would resign; Károlyi would remain President and name a Social Democratic cabinet, which should refuse the demands of the Vyx note.

Before making the decision, the government was not familiar with some of the new developments. The Soldiers' Council, upon the suggestion of Chairman Pogány, decided that the armed forces would support the Communists. At five o'clock in the afternoon, the automobiles of the ministers were confiscated, and the Budapest garrison was under communist command. In the Workers' Council, Sándor Garbai declared that a Soviet (Council) government would be formed. A newspaperman, Paul Kéri, visited Károlyi later that night and asked him to revise his standpoint and resign.

Károlyi honestly believed that his country was falling apart and did not resist when the newly formed Communist-Socialist coalition, headed by Béla Kun, grabbed power. Many people shared his opinion on the inevitable military, political and economic consequences of the Vyx note, including many of those who did not like Károlyi's leftist convictions. An American observer vividly described the situation that had arisen:

> "In February, 1919, the Peace Conference announced preliminary boundries for Hungary which gave Slovakia, Serbia and Rumania chunks of undoubtedly Hungarian population and denuded her of industrial and agricultural areas vital to national existence. This at once gave impulse to communist agitation and greatly weakened the Károlyi regime. Károlyi apparently got the notion if the country went Bolshevik it would frighten the Peace Conference."[32]

Mihály Károlyi's attempt to heal all of Hungary's ills by ending the war, sweeping away the outdated political and social system, cutting the link with the Habsburgs and the Germans, calming the nationalities and gaining the sympathy of the Entente, failed completely. He had the right goal but

33

chose the wrong means. Overestimating his capacities and under-rating his enemies he lost the risky political game which he initiated during the war. His fall discredited the policies of the Károlyi party as well as many democratic principles. The nation, at least a significant part of the urban population, turned to Kun and Soviet Russia, having lost interest in the Wilsonian principles and the Allied promises which proved to be phony.

V. SOVIET HUNGARY

The circumstances of the establishment of the proletarian dictatorship are still not clear. Károlyi in his *Memoirs* denied that he signed the abdication document. His widow declared in a letter to the editor of a historical magazine that Károlyi returned the draft to his secretary with the remark: "I will not sign this."[33] Böhm confirmed that Károlyi's name was used on the published proclamation without his consent. On the other hand, D. Berinkey, the Prime Minister of the People's Republic, stated in a testimony in court that he saw the original abdication document, signed by Károlyi.[34]

Whether Károlyi resigned or not, the power slipped to the Soviets, who sought Russian help immediately. Lenin was eager to support his Hungarian comrades, but at the same time Admiral Kolchak's troops launched a powerful offensive against the Russian Red Army, and in April war broke out between Russia and Poland, too. A government telegram sent to the *Leipziger Volkszeitung* stated that the Communists in Budapest were not afraid of Allied military intervention, because in that case "the proletariat of the whole world would line up behind Hungary," although it was quite obvious that the time was not ripe for a global socialist revolution.[35] The Sovietization of Central Europe on the other hand was not a too distant possibility. Internal unrest increased in the Successor States as well as in Austria and Germany. Marshal

34

Foch presented a plan at the March 27th meeting of the Council of Four in Paris, which set as a goal the "organization of a barrier against Bolshevism." He did not advocate offensive action, only some kind of a demarcation line behind which the Allies could proceed to clean up the region. Foch insisted that Vienna should be occupied to ensure the safety of their lines of communication with Poland and Rumania, since five days before the meeting a communist regime was established in Hungary.

President Wilson and Britain's Lloyd George opposed any intervention. The only way to take action against Bolshevism, Wilson said, was to eliminate its causes.[36] Finally, the Allied and Associated Powers, who were quite unwilling to negotiate seriously with Károlyi,[37] sent General J. C. Smuts to Budapest, after they learned that the Kun regime ordered the establishment of a Red Guard and a Red Army.

The General arrived in Budapest on April 4th and immediately invited the People's Commissars to his train, which he never left during his visit. President Garbai of the Soviet Republic, Commissars Kun and Kunfi, and the Vienna envoy of the Soviets, Bolgár represented Hungary. During the negotiations Smuts emphasized that he brought with him the very last proposals of the victorious states, "who wanted to live in peace with Hungary and secure the appropriate internal development of the country." The Hungarian standpoint was very similar to that expressed by A. A. Joffe, the head of the Soviet Russian delegation at the Brest-Litovsk peace conference in December, 1917: Peace without annexations and indemnities, and the right of self-determination for all nationalities living in Hungary. As Kun said later, Hungary had been "too weak to negotiate;"[38] therefore the proposal of the Allies was not too unreasonable under the circumstances.

The Entente suggested the drawing of the new demarcation line between the Hungarian and Rumanian armies five to thirteen miles east of that of the Vyx ultimatum, and the establishment of a wide neutral zone which was supposed to be occupied by English, French, Italian and possibly American troops. The March 20th note gave important cities such as Debrecen, Hódmezővásárhely, Szeged, Makó and Orosháza to the Rumanians; the new proposal returned them to Hungary.

Smuts solemnly declared that the new demarcation line would not influence the determination of the final borders of Hungary, promised the termination of the Allied blockade, and indicated that the Hungarian Soviet government would be invited to the Peace Conference. He finally suggested a meeting with other nations of the former Monarchy.

The South African General especially wanted to "fix an armistice line between the Hungarians and Rumanians, yet the real idea at the back [was] to see whether Béla Kun was worth using as a vehicle for getting into touch with Moscow."[39] In spite of this, Kun's position was considerably strengthened by the visit, which he believed was a "de facto" recognition of his government by the Allies and an expression of willingness on the part of the Peace Conference to negotiate with him.

Kun's final offer was considered excessive and was refused by Smuts, who left for Prague the next day. The Hungarian Soviet government had new plans then.

Tibor Számuelly, Vice-Commissar for Defense, ordered the organization of "front-line propaganda" on April 6th, hoping that the Czech and Rumanian troops would not oppose a proletarian army. His instructions were based on the communist nucleus of the armed forces:

> At each battalion the political commissar of the regiment selects one comrade from among the party stewards for propaganda. He can select men for patrol as the need arises. The leader of the patrol must be a very reliable comrade. The strength of the patrols will be about 10 men. Non-military personnel may be used for propaganda upon the recommendation of the local party organization. Those comrades who are in charge of propaganda activities, cannot be used for any other duty.

Propagandists were subordinated to divisional commanders only; they remained at the operational area even after the replacement of their units.

The "spreading of communist ideology and the call for rebellion against their own imperialists"[40] was not successful, although some Rumanian soldiers turned against their commanders and near the city of Makó, Serbian troops threw away their weapons and gave up plans for the occupation of an important bridge.[41] Such occurences generally did not have a political background and nationalistic territory-grabbing proved to be the victorious ideology, in spite of temporary communist military successes.

At the beginning of the Rumanian military intervention, the army of the Hungarian Republic of Councils consisted of quite undisciplined, politically oriented units most of which were organized by the Károlyi regime. Kun and his comrades dissolved the Soldiers' Councils right after the takeover, not bothering about the important role which they played in the overthrow of the People's Republic. Political Commissars were appointed, and Revolutionary Military Courts were established. Workers' battalions and international brigades were sent to the front.

Until the end of April, seven Rumanian divisions, more than 50,000 soldiers, fought against numerically weaker Red Army units. On April 20th the invaders reached Nagyvárad (Oradea Mare) and three days later they occupied Debrecen.

Newly formed regiments were sent to the eastern front from Budapest and other industrial cities, and on May 3 the Hungarian Red Army dispersed the Rumanians at Szolnok and stopped their advance at the Tisza river.

At the same time the Czech attack also came to a standstill. On May 10 a Hungarian counter-attack drove the enemy behind the Ipoly River and consolidated the position of the Red Army in Northern Hungary. Later in June, the Czech troops had to be withdrawn by 40-100 miles as the result of a Hungarian offensive.

The Hungarian Soviets were not too modest in reoccupied

areas. The newly established tiny Slovak Soviet Republic was supposed to soon deliver 30,000 wagons of food and wood to Budapest.[42]

Among the important changes that characterized the home rule of the communist regime was the nationalization of industrial enterprises and mines employing more than 20 workers. Foreign commerce, apartment buildings, and big stores as well as farms larger than 100 cadestral yokes (about 57 hectares) were also taken over by the state. As a result of the radical reorganization of the economy, chaos and restlessness developed.

Popular reforms, such as the introduction of 8-hour work days, free medical services, lower rents and wage increases could not pacify the country.

To counter the increasing activities of anti-Communist elements, terrorist groups traveled around in armored trains and executed many counter-revolutionaries, together with innocent people denounced by their enemies. Most of the victims were farmers, public servants and former officers, but workers were also dragged before the revolutionary courts if they resisted the measures of the government. The maintenance of public order was one of the difficult tasks. Soldiers of the Red Army were frequently sentenced for robberies and other common crimes.

There was no unity in the Socialist Party of Hungary, the name of which was later changed to Party of Socialist-Communist Workers of Hungary. On May 2 moderate socialist leaders (Manó Buchinger, Gyula Peidl, Jenő Weltner and others) openly demanded the liquidation of the Soviet regime. The June 14-23 meeting of the National Assembly of Councils also proved the irreconcilable contradiction between the views of the leaders of the traditional workers' party and the Communists. The Social Democrats were ready to make ideological sacrifices in order to secure agricultural and industrial production, but Kun and his comrades were unwilling to give up one iota of their program, in spite of the warnings of Lenin himself. In his March 23 message Lenin emphasized that "the simple imitation of our Russian tactic would be a mistake."

When foreign intervention began on April 16, the socialist leaders lined up behind the Soviet government almost without exception. Kunfi, Haubrich and Pogány, who represented the center in the new government, all voted in favor of military resistance at the April 18 meeting of the Revolutionary Governing Council. Zsigmond Kunfi called for the realization of the dictatorship of the proletariat one day later at the meeting of the Budapest Workers' Council. "Today," he said, "the unity, fighting spirit and power of the proletariat against this bourgeois attack can be secured only if we enforce all of those demands which are the necessary results of the dictatorship of the proletariat."[43]

In spite of his political stiffness, Béla Kun also had to make concessions in order to secure the loyalty of the Socialists who represented the majority of the governing groups. The composition of the government was changed; People's Commissar Számuelly was sent to the front line; the propaganda which was directed mainly against the neighboring capitalist countries was cut down, and the concept of political prisoner was re-introduced.

One of the Commissars, Péter Ágoston told an American visitor (Prof. Brown) on April 24 that he and some of his comrades intended to send Kun to Switzerland, which would have given an opportunity for the formation of a new moderate government. Brown reported the conversation to A. C. Coolidge in Vienna who did not find it realistic. America was not in a position to support Ágoston in any way.

On May 1 huge mass meetings and demonstrations were organized all over the country. At the same time the Rumanian troops reached the right bank of the Tisza river, threatening the capitol city itself. In this critical situation anti-Communists as well as opportunists and vacillating neophytes started a concentrated attack against the regime. In the late hours of May 1 non-Bolshevist members of the Governing Council and trade union leaders suggested to "transfer the power to

39

a Directorium recruited from among the workers which — maintaining all of the economic and other mesures that will lead to socialism — will be in charge of administration for the duration of the period necessary for the transition from the dictatorship of the proletariat to the dictatorship of the bourgeoise."

Béla Kun reviewed the proposal at the May 2 meeting of the Governing Council, admitting that the fighting ability of the troops was equal to zero. Still he did not consider the situation entirely hopeless, stated that the Governing Council "should not give up" and called on the Hungarian proletariat to "stand up [against the invaders] to the very last man."

Bokányi believed that a "mixed Directorium" should take over the government, hoping that the Allies would be willing to negotiate with it. In Kunfi's opinion a new group composed by the representatives of the workers should govern. It should release the political prisoners, abolish censorship and ask the Austrian Socialists to mediate between Hungary and the Entente powers.

In the meantime, the Allies in Paris conducted negotiations about the elimination of the communist menace from Central Europe. The *cordon sanitaire,* proposed by Clemenceau, was not enough. Marshall Foch declared on July 17th, at secret negotiations in the Villa Majestic in Paris, that "to liberate Hungary from communism in one week, a force of 8 infantry divisions, one cavalry division, 100 aeroplanes and as many armoured cars as possible would suffice." The Marshal learned from intelligence sources that the Red Army was composed of 9 divisions, one of which, the 4th infantry division had been disbanded. "Each division could only muster a small number of rifles. For instance, the 9th division had only 2,000 to 3,000 rifles."[44]

There was some disagreement among the Allied powers in regard to armed intervention. Balfour said at the meeting that "the very remarkable" report of Marshall Foch made him apprehensive. He referred to the passage in which Foch alluded the necessity of establishing in Hungary a government

40

with which the Entente could negotiate peace. "Such a government would not appear to be a Hungarian Government, but one set up by the Entente Powers. The Peace would be represented for all time not between the Powers and the Hungarian people, but as a Peace between the Powers and their own puppets."

Tittoni, the representative of Italy, represented a different position. In his view "the Hungarian situation was a difficult one. Hungary was ruled by a small minority, 80 per cent of the Hungarian troops were against Béla Kun..."

Nine days later the Allied and Associated Governments stated in a declaration that they were anxious to sign a peace treaty:

> with a government which represented the Hungarian people and not with one that rests its authority upon terrorism. Foreign occupation of Hungarian territory, as defined by the Peace Conference, will cease as soon as the terms of the armistice... have been satisfactorily complied with.[45]

As it turned out, leading politicians in France were considering the complete destruction of Hungary,[46] although others were averse even to breaking up Austria-Hungary, which played an important role in the European balance of power.[47]

Preceding the secret meeting Marshal Foch and representatives of Czechoslovakia and Yugoslavia conferred with members of the Supreme Council of the Peace Conference on the forces available for use against the Hungarian Soviet government. France objected to proposals according to which she was supposed to furnish the bulk of the expeditionary army. Newspaper reports indicated on July 16 that General Franchet d'Esperey sent an ultimatum to Béla Kun threatening to occupy Budapest unless he resigned.

On May 2nd, 1919, two employees of the Hungarian Legation in Vienna broke into the room of Envoy Elek Bolgár, who was in Budapest. They found 135 million Hungarian crowns, 98,000 Swiss francs and 333,000 French francs, which were destined to support foreign revolutionary movements. (The larger part of the amount reached the Szeged counter-revolutionary government in early June. Horthy recalled, "couriers from Vienna had brought us money, appropriated from the Communist Hungarian Legation in a bold *coup de main* by a group of Hungarian officers under the blind eye of the friendly Viennese Chief of Police Schober, and with the aid of the Vienna correspondent of the *Daily Telegraph.")* The opposition to the revolutionary regime strengthened, but there were favorable signs also. About the same time that Count Gyula Károlyi's counter-revolutionary government was formed in Szeged, which belonged to the French zone of occupation, Kun received news that Allied recognition of his government was expected. His June 9th note to Alizé, the head of the French mission in Vienna, joyously acknowledged the forthcoming invitation to the Paris Peace Conference.[48] The glimmer of hope was actually earlier extinguished by the June 7th ultimatum of Clemenceau, in which he demanded the stop of "unjustifiable" attacks of the Hungarian Red Army against the Czechs. On June 10th, Kun promised to stop the hostilities, but on June 11th French troops arrived at Pozsony (Bratislava) anyhow.

In June Prince Lajos Windischgraetz had a conference with Aristide Briand, the French Minister for Foreign Affairs in a Paris restaurant. "As I understand it," Briand said, "the Emperor is interested in an operation which, though not of a legitimist character, is taking shape at Szeged against the Béla Kun regime. Well, what is it that you want?"

Windischgraetz replied that it was a matter of providing arms for a few thousand Hungarian officers and soldiers who assembled at Szeged and were under the command of Admiral Horthy. Briand nodded assent.[49]

Internal difficulties were also growing. The Communists did not distribute the land to the peasants, but nationalized it and set the starving urban population against the government by confiscations, arrests and red tape. The majority of the production commissioners who sat in the offices of former factory managers were ignorant and ineffective. Soon the output of mines decreased by 15-38 per cent in comparison to the first months of the year, although coal was desperately needed because of the loss of mining areas to the Czechs and Rumanians. In factories productivity also declined dangerously. By the end of April, railway service was reduced. Meat, lard, flour, bread, sugar, wood and coal were rationed. Decrees socialized private libraries, works of art, jewelry, pianos, Oriental rugs, bicycles, microscopes, and stamp collections. Private bathrooms were to be made available to members of an assigned proletarian family on Saturday nights. The general confusion was characterized by a statement which denied rumors that women would be made common property of men ("die Frauen nicht communisieren wird...").[50] The forced retreat from the northern front, after initial victories, demoralized the troops and the commanders, many of whom joined the Red Army for patriotic reasons.

Károly Peyer, a former Social Democratic party leader and an official of the Kun government, issued a statement on June 21st in connection with the newly established frontiers of Hungary making it clear that they meant a death sentence for the country.[51] His opinion evidently reflected the thinking of the regime, and the situation became very similar to that which forced Károlyi in March to abandon the helm. Earlier, on June 12th, the increase of counter-revolutionary movements was acknowledged by the authorities, too. Kun believed that the constantly arriving Clemenceau telegrams were signs of an "imperialistic Götterdaemmerung," but words were not effective enough to stop the enemy offensive.

On June 24 cadets of the national Ludovika Military Academy in Budapest organized an armed uprising and marched against government buildings under the command of some of their officers. Simultaneously Danube river-gunboats opened fire on the Hungaria Hotel which was the headquarters of the Soviet leaders and the residence for their families. Riots also started in Transdanubian villages and towns, which proved that the counter-revolutionaries were centrally organized and directed. The uprising was quelled quickly; the execution of forty cadets was prevented by Entente protests, but others, especially in the countryside, were hanged.

The result of the June uprisings threw cold water on many hesitant leaders of the Social Democratic Party. They felt that they were right from the beginning in opposing the fusion with the Communists and blamed Kun for the troop withdrawals from the North, particularly when it became evident that the June 13 note of Clemenceau in which he promised the retreat of the Rumanian army in return for the evacuation of Slovakia was nothing but diversionary tactics.

Vilmos Böhm, the former Commander-in-Chief of the Red Army, was appointed Minister Plenipotentiary to Austria in July. He was hesitant to represent the Soviet Government abroad apparently because a mandate to negotiate with the Allies was among his instructions, but his socialist friends, Kunfi, Garbai and Weltner convinced him that he might be able to save the regime and his mission was not that of a gravedigger.

On July 23 the Allied representatives presented to Böhm a memorandum which contained the following proposals according to Böhm's *Memoirs:*

1. A dictatorial regime should take over the power. It would be advisable to include the following men in the government: Haubrich, Ágoston and Garami.
2. Kun's Communist government must be expelled, Bolshevism must be eliminated. Bolshevik propaganda should stop.
3. The dictatorship should be temporary and serve as a provisionary measure for the organization of a new government which will represent all social classes.
4. All kinds of terroristic action, confiscation and seizure should stop immediately.
5. The new government should invite to Budapest an Allied Council which will support its program.
6. The blockade will be dissolved; the Allies will take measures for the transportation of food and coal to Hungary and for the support of the re-opening of Danube shipping.

7. Every form of political persecution must stop.
8. The permanent government should make the final decision in regard to socialization [of private property].

Böhm was not to be included in the new government because of his former role in the Soviet party and military apparatus, but he accepted the proposal on a temporary basis. Two other formerly Socialist party leaders Weltner and Peyer, also approved it when they arrived in Viennt on July 24. As Peyer stated later at the organizational meeting of the new Social Democratic Party in August, "the negotiations in Vienna . . . convinced us that communism in Hungary was doomed to failure."

Earlier, on July 10, the Red Army started a new, embittered campaign against the Rumanians. The Hungarian forces consisted of 78 infantry divisions, 3 cavalry divisions and 91 artillery batteries. The Rumanian army had 92 infantry divisions and 58 cavalry divisions[52] which were much better equipped than the Hungarian army. In addition to their overwhelming strength the plans of the offensive were passed over to the hands of the Rumanians through the Szeged group. Red Army Chief of Staff Julier sent them to Captain Gömbös, who was Deputy Minister of Defense in the counter-revolutionary government.

The Hungarian Red Army could not expect much help from the Russian Soviet government which in May stopped the Rumanian advance by an ultimatum. In spite of the Rumanian military superiority the Hungarian units crossed the Tisza river and forced the enemy to retreat until July 23, but on July 24 the Rumanians took over the initiative. On July 30 they established beachheads on the right bank of the Tisza and their advancement toward Budapest could no longer be checked. The Hungarian Red Army, demoralized earlier by the forced retreat in the north, streamed back disorderly.

On July 31 the military situation became critical. The Royal Rumanian Army started a concentrated attack along the entire frontline. At night the 6th Rumanian Division stood one mile from Szolnok, a key city at the Tisza river, and other troops occupied Tokaj and Tarcal in the north.

Colonel Julier, the Chief of Staff of the Hungarian Red Army, who was a non-communist professional officer, saw that time was ripe for replacing the Kun government with a national regime. He sent a report to War Commissar Landler, in which he described the position of Hungarian forces as "hopeless." In his opinion the threatening occupation of Budapest could be avoided only if the Red Army could force the enemy back in the Szolnok area. If the counter-attack were unsuccessful, "law and order would break up in Budapest and the Entente would intervene from every direction," according to the report. "All symptoms indicate that the troops are not disciplined and do not posses the necessary moral values. Under such circumstances there is no guarantee for the successful leadership of the army."

As a commissar told the leaders of the Iron and Metalworkers' Union on May 2nd, "there were no weapons, food or uniforms; the troops were undisciplined, looked like a mob." The situation did not improve later, although many workers were willing to fight for the Soviets to the end. Finally, at the August 1st session of the Central Workers' Council, the Kun government[53] surrendered its diminishing power to a moderate group consisting of union leaders.

According to the speech of Commissar Zoltán Rónai to the 500-member Workers' Council which served as the parliament of the Hungarian Soviet regime, the leaders of the Hungarian proletariat built their hopes in March on three possibilities: the quick spreading of the world revolution, the help of the Soviet-Russian army and the self-sacrifice of the Hungarian proletariat. As it turned out, none of these conditions was present "as it was expected" then. He emphasized that "if the majority of the proletariat would have supported the dictatorship, then we would have been able to wait for the spreading of the world revolution and the advance of the Russian army," adding that the majority of the proletariat did not want to fight.

Describing the military situation Rónai explained that the

Rumanian front collapsed. "Even if we could beat [them] back temporarily, our resistance would not be permanent considering the present status of our armed forces." If the workers would die on the barricades, the international workers' movement would lose too, because its Hungarian leaders would be exterminated. "The Entente," he said, "gained victory without decisively beating us, because the masses did not show a determined resistance."

The future was rather cloudy in Rónai's opinion. "It is more likely that we can finish our struggle in a decent way if we negotiate at a time when we are not completely beaten and crushed as if we continue fighting until our complete destruction." His conclusion was that the war against the Rumanians was lost and "the dictatorship of the proletariat, by the will of the majority of the proletarians, has fallen, although I hope that this is not final, only a temporary development."

The Revolutionary Governing Council and the party leaders had already agreed that resignation was the only way out. Earlier — after Kun's speech — Számuelly and Commissar Hamburger objected to the idea, but at the plenary session Rónai's proposals were accepted unanimously without any debate.[54]

The last speech was delivered by István Biermann who emphasized that not everything was lost. "We will come back," he said, "and the proletariat will take over again. The Workers' Councils must continue their work, everybody should work without any interruption and contribute to the maintenance of order in these terrible times. Prevent everywhere the emergence of the white counter-revolution."

After the meeting some of the best known communist leaders such as Ottó Korvin, György Lukács and József Révai left their homes and were hiding from the new authorities which they helped to organize. Béla Kun learned that night that he and some others received political asylum from the Austrian government.

It belongs to the antecedents that Kun visited the city of

47

Cegléd in Central Hungary on July 31st, and realized that a military collapse could not be prevented. At night in Cegléd an impromptu War Council ordered a counter-offensive in spite of the hopeless situation, and at another conference held later in Budapest the Communists demanded the total mobilization of the workers and the continuation of the fighting, but the general mood of the armed forces did not favor such ventures. The army units stationed in Budapest were at that time under the influence of Social Democrats and professional officers. The July 26th statement of the Allies (quoted earlier) was another clear warning to Kun. On July 22 Vilmos Böhm, the Hungarian envoy to Austria in the latter part of the 133 day rule of the Soviets, informed Colonel Cuninghame, the British military representative in Vienna, that Kun expressed willingness to withdraw if the Socialists were acceptable to the Allies.[55] (Austria was the only country which recognized the Hungarian Soviet government.) The July 13th radio telegram of the Peace Conference made it clear that the Big Four did not want to negotiate with Kun, because "the Soviets did not keep the armistice stipulations."

General dissatisfaction with the government further increased in Budapest as well as in the countryside. The farmers were unwilling to sell their products for the new white banknotes (so called because one side of the bills were left blank); they practically starved out the cities. It was evident that the days of the communist regime were numbered.

Kun's proclamation issued on July 31st to the proletariat of the world was a last frantic effort to reverse the situation. He complained in it about the starvation of Hungarians, which was the result of the Allied blockade, and stated that Balkan hordes were released against his people in the name of high cultural ideals. Just like the June 15th proclamation of the Hungarian communist leaders to the French proletariat in which they asked for assistance "against the international counter-revolution of Versailles," this was also without result and the expected world proletarian solidarity did not materialize. The only result was the protest of a Socialist conference in Lucerne, Switzerland against Entente policy on August 9.

Béla Kun and his associates arrived by special train to Vienna in the early hours of August 2nd. As it was mentioned earlier, upon the request of Böhm, the Austrian Socialist government gave political asylum to the Kun group in advance.[56] One train took Kun, Jenő Landler and others to Vienna. Another carried the rest of the escaping People's Commissars and their families. On the way to the railroad station anti-communist crowds assembled, rocks and curses were flying and somebody shot Landler's daughter, who was seated with him in an automobile. The fall of the Hungarian Soviet government was final; the way was open for Gyula Peidl and his social democratic comrades.

VI. THE TRADE UNION GOVERNMENT

The chances of the Peidl *ministerium* were not very promising, mainly because it included four former Commissars, who were suddenly transformed again into Social Democrats. Three of them received important portfolios: Péter Ágoston became the Minister of Foreign Affairs, Sándor Garbai took over the Ministry of Culture and Education, and József Haubrich was named Minister of Defense. Prime Minister Peidl was the leader of the Printers' Union from the turn of the century. In 1909 he became a member of the leading body of the Social Democratic Party of Hungary. During the months of Károlyi's People's Republic, Peidl was the Minister of Labor and Welfare. He opposed the union with the Communists and resigned his post in the party, but kept his membership in the new Communist-Socialist party organization. When emissaries of the Governing Council informed Peidl that he was appointed Minister President, he went to the party club where Garbai, the President of the Hungarian Soviet Republic, gave him the list of the members of the new cabinet. Peidl first didn't want to include those in his government "who were People's Commissars one day ago" mainly because the new regime had to stand on the basis of private property and bourgeois values. The Prime Minister was unwilling to participate at the session of the Central Workers' Council, therefore its decisions were not obligatory for him.

Peyer, the new Minister of the Interior — traditionally the most influential position in the cabinet — did not side wholeheartedly with Kun; therefore, some members of the Workers' Council wanted him to be dropped from Rónai's list, but time was pressing and there was no opposition when voting came. On the other hand, the composition of the government seemed to be an exercise in futility for the non-comunist forces, and gave rise to the suspicion that Peidl was a proconsul of Kun.

Peidl immediately asked Böhm to visit the representatives of the Great Powers in Vienna. Böhm declared in the presence of the British Cuninghame, the Italian Prince Borghese and the French Alizé that the new Hungarian regime stood on the basis of democratic freedom, would hold free elections, recognized the November 13th, 1918 armistice agreement, invalidated all terroristic rules and regulations, and intended to restore law and order. Böhm also visited Captain Thomas C. Gregory of the American Military Mission and asked him to intervene in connection with the lifting of the blockade. Gregory asked the Hungarians to send a fully authorized economic expert to Vienna and promised his support.

A government Manifesto addressed to "the people of Hungary" and published in the Social Democratic daily *Népszava* on August 2 referred to the mandate that was given to Peidl by the Budapest Central Council of Workers and Soliders, which indicated continuity. It also mentioned the July 28 declaration of the Paris Peace Conference that stipulated the formation of a new government based on the people's will as a pre-requisite for peace negotiations. The Manifesto insinuated that the Peidl government met such requirements, and

stated that it depended on the strength of the class-conscious organized workers. "The new government trusts that the unionized workers will not tolerate the ravages of counter-revolutionaries and plunderers. It intends to protect the people of Hungary from the destruction of the white terror and the horror of mob actions. Knowing that the working masses stand in close-ranked formations behind the government, it asks the people of Hungary to wait for the evolution of events in a disciplined way and obey the orders of the government under any circumstances." The last statement revealed that the position of the government was far from being settled and the new cabinet anticipated disturbances. To increase optimism the Manifesto remarked that "there is no reason for defeatism. The front line at the Tisza river is firmly held."

In reality armed resistance was tottering. The soldiers dispersed from the barracks in all directions. The Albrecht Garrison in Budapest was empty; the sailors and officers of the "Marx" gunboat left their barracks, the soldiers of the 2nd infantry regiment which was composed of ironworkers, went home. The international brigades from the Bebel barracks escaped toward the Austrian border. Adherents of the Republic of Councils knew that communism in Hungary was irretrievably lost.

The telegram of the Central Secretariat of the Social Democratic party, which was sent to county party organizations, referred to the agreement with the Entente in connection with the formation of the trade union goverment and instructed the administrative organs of the workers to continue their work. In order to restore domestic tranquility the telegram held out the prospect of martial law.

War Minister Haubrich informed the armed forces about the change in government and ordered the commanders to seek contact with enemy troop commands and tell them that "since a new government was formed in Hungary today in accordance with the wishes of the Entente and the necessary steps were taken for an armistice agreement, the fighting must stop." The order assured the army corps commanders and subordinate officers that they would continue to be in command, adding that "the political commissaries also stay for the time being and should make an effort to put across the change without trouble."

The order was the result of negotiations with Colonel Romanelli, who asked Clemenceau in a telegram to order an armistice as soon as possible between the Allied armies and the Hungarian army and to stop the advance of the Allied armies.

The Rumanian armies occupied Füzesabony, an important railroad junction, on August 1 and cut the railroad line between Budapest and Miskolc, although other Rumanian units were contained in the Szolnok area and the Tisza defense line was still standing.

The first meeting of the new Council of Ministers started on August 2nd with the abolition of the Hungarian Soviet Republic and the re-establishment of the People's Republic. Peidl and his colleagues dissolved the revolutionary courts, confirmed the traditional judiciary system, and set free all anti-Communists and hostages who had been imprisoned by Soviet authorities.[57] The amnesty decree essentially established the illegality of communist criminal procedures by stating that "if sentence was passed on the case the punishment will be void and all of the legal consequences will expire." This also meant that the legal system of the fallen regime was outlawed. The release of the political prisoners strengthened the counter-revolutionary forces and substantiated the rumors about the approaching day of reckoning. The Council of Ministers also decided to release immediately former Ministers Sándor Wekerle, József Szterényi, Samu Hazai and Sándor Szurmay, some of whom were interned by the Károlyi-Berinkey government. They were made partially responsible for the bloodshed and misery of the World War by the political left during the Károlyi era.

In spite of such measures, the behavior of a large part of the population was ominous. Several state and city employees were insulting the new Ministers; some of the cabinet members were afraid to enter their offices. Smaller units of the Red Army deserted to Horthy, and the ever present opportunists who just days ago supported the Soviet government, now started a campaign against Peidl, who courageously resisted when others were ducking.

The Prime Minister sent a telegram on August 2nd to István Nagyatádi Szabó, the leader of the centrist Smallholders' Party, inviting him to participate in the work of the cabinet, and asked Catholic prelate Sándor Giesswein, a well known pacifist politician. who was one of the founders of the Christian Socialist movement in Hungary, to accept one of the portfolios. As the result of such steps, Colonel Romanelli, the Chairman of the Allied Military Mission, promised the termination of the blockade.

Good news came from the front line, too. The Hungarian army — still called red — gained an unexpected victory on August 2nd and reoccupied the key city of Szolnok from the Rumanians.[58]

The Allies ordered Romanelli to initiate negotiations with Peidl, stipulating that the latter should recognize the conditions of the November 3, 1918 armistice. Peidl was willing to comply, and used the opportunity to submit a request for an international army of occupation, partly as a balance against the Rumanians and Czechs, but mainly because he needed it as a support for his unstable government.

Romanelli demanded the organization of a small professional army and the disbanding of the Red Guard, stating that "the presence of the Royal Rumanian Army makes it unnecessary for the new Hungarian government to keep separate armed forces for the maintenance of peace and legality." The August 5 decree of the Minister of War was basically a writ for the execution of Romanelli's demand. It ordered the disarming of military units, with the exception of professional soldiers. Rifles, bayonets and ammunition had to be stored in safe places. "Armed squads of commissioned and non-commissioned officers must be formed at the barracks. The obligation of these squads will be the maintenance of public order and the disarming [of the soldiers] with the help of the gendarmery, customs police and the old city police which have been set up again. The commander of the armed squads must be a determined professional officer."

"The organization of these squads is the most urgent task. In Budapest the district command, elsewhere the garrison commander or the ranking army or gendarmery officers will be in charge of the organization of the units."

"All terrorist bands and individual terrorists must be disarmed at once; in case of disobedience they should be shot to death on the spot. If political or army commissars would be found, they should be dismissed immediately."

The disbanding of the Red Guard was just a recognition of the facts, because the Guard was already atomized and crippled by the escape of its commanders. The city and village Soviets lost their armed support and although formally they were still in charge of the local administration, the anti-communist officer corps could remove them more or less legally.

Peidl and Peyer ordered the capture of the escaping exponents of the communist system, too.[59] According to a confidential telegram of the Ministry of the Interior which was sent to every country administrator, "the escape of the Communists should be prevented. Escapees should be arrested." Other telegrams earlier instructed employees of the district administrations and the Red Guard to capture exponents of the former regime, many of whom escaped to Austria "with large amounts of money." A thorough investigation of passengers of trains, automobiles and other vehicles was ordered in areas near the Austrian border.

Among those arrested were three members of the Central Committee of the communist youth organization, detectives and investigators of terrorist groups, political commissars, and members of the Budapest city Soviet, whose names and activities were not known by most people. Ottó Korvin was the only significant communist leader in prison. He was one

of the founders of the party, and during the Soviet era became the chief of the political department of the Commissariat for Internal Affairs. Terrorist teams (the so called Lenin Boys) organized by Korvin participated in a number of atrocities in Budapest as well as in the countryside.[60]

A government decree dated August 4th invalidated the socialization of apartment buildings and reinstated the old rental regulations; on August 5th the so-called blue banknotes of the former Monarchy were re-introduced instead of the white bills of the Soviet government. Another decree issued on August 7th abolished all Soviet institutions and restored private property in industry and commerce. Property rights in agriculture were also re-established and the government compelled farmers and land owners to secure the continuity of agricultural production.

All of these steps were meaningless in the opinion of the increasing anti-communist organizations. Leaders of some conservative groups which included royalists, army officers, Catholics, landowners and farmers wanted revenge and the complete restoration of legal continuation with Archduke Joseph Habsburg at the helm.[61] Joseph praised Károlyi's republic in 1918 and was among the first to take the required oath, but this was no longer an obstacle. Emissaries of the royalist right, led by István Friedrich, a machine manufacturer, visited the hesitant Archduke at his castle and took him to Budapest, on the night of August 4th.

Friedrich's political career was quite eventful. He spent eight years in the United States as a workingman before the World War. In 1914 he accompanied Károlyi to America, and in 1918 became Assistant War Minister in the first Károlyi cabinet. In Károlyi's opinion, Friedrich was "an uncontrollable demagogue." He was the one who on the eve of the October 1918 populist revolution urged the excited crowd to storm the palace of the King's representative to force Károlyi's nomination. Friedrich was leftist and internationalist then, but one year later became the leader of the royalist counter-revolution. His organization included András

Csilléry, a dentist, Jakab Bleyer, a university professor, General Ferenc Schnetzer, Károly Rassay, a well known liberal politician, writer Gyula Pekár, and several officers and civil servants. They were plotting to overthrow the proletarian dictatorship for months.[62]

Counter-revolutionary elements realized that time was ripe for action on August 1, when members of the "White House" group led by Friedrich and Csilléry held their first meeting. They decided to depose the Peidl government. On August 2 post office workers and employees of the city hall organized meetings at which they sang the national anthem and expressed their joy about the fall of communism. There were meetings in front of military barracks and the Hotel Ritz where an enthusiastic crowd cheered Colonel Romanelli. Speakers demanded the restoration of the Kingdom of Hungary and the punishment of those who were responsible for the red terror.

The deposal of the Peidl government was scheduled for August 5th. One of the reasons for the feverish haste was a telegram that was sent to Peidl by Böhm from Vienna. He stated in it that "the agreement with the Entente is ready. If you will include four bourgeois and two peasants in your government, we will continue to be in charge."[63] From this and the conference between Peidl and middle-class politicians such as Nagyatádi Szabo, Giesswein and Károly Huszár, the Friedrich group drew the conclusion that a coalition government was in the making and they could probably not get Rumanian help for its removal if they didn't act swiftly.

The plan of the coup d'etat was discussed with Colonel Romanelli, who opposed it. General Vasilescu, the Chief of Staff of the Rumanian army, approved the plan but threatened with armed intervention if the conspirators would not grab the power at once and confusion resulted. The Rumanians believed that the Peidl ministry "was not to be trusted," according to an August 5, 1919 report of the *New York Times*.

On the same day the Social Democratic daily *Népszava* indicated that the situation was worsening for the workers'

movement. "The Hungarian proletariat is surprised to see," it said, "that in spite of the magnificent sacrifices it is on a collision course again with those who made well organized work impossible here, who institutionalized loafing, and opposed any trend which wanted to eliminate Tartarian methods from European civilization. Those who started the war and incited it appeared on the horizon again... and want to break law and order by threats and grinding their teeth in exasperation, hoping to swing into the saddle." The Minister of War warned the irresponsible elements of the bourgeoise but also turned against the former political commissars who "acting in the name of the workers but having subversive intentions, use the tense atmosphere to spread different hair-raising rumors to cause alarm among the population."

In Vienna, Counts György Pallavicini and István Csáky repeatedly asked Rumania, through her diplomatic representative, to seize the Hungarian capital. Finally upon the request of General Schnetzer, the Rumanians occupied Budapest on August 4th, in spite of several Allied warnings.[64] Complete chaos in the unoccupied part of Hungary provided another reason for foreign intervention. During the first week of August, the communist administration came to an end and the old authorities had not yet taken over. Pillaging and punitive actions of individuals made the restoration of public order very difficult. The occupation was going quite smoothly. The population of Budapest was lethargic after so many changes in government; there was no organized resistance. Soon arrests of suspected Communists, rape, murder, robbery and other atrocities became the order of the day. Foreign military missions received several complaints every day about the intolerable behavior of the Rumanians. Even Allied military personnel were not spared. On August 25th American marine Hargraves was arrested by a Rumanian patrol for an unknown reason, and on November 18th Rumanians opened fire on a British Danube warship, which returned the fire and wounded a Rumanian soldier.[65]

Dr. Munro of the British Food Commission and the Swiss

Captain Brunier of the International Red Cross visited a number of towns occupied by the Rumanians and issued a statement in telegraphic style on their finding in Oct. 1919:

> *In all towns occupied by Rumanians, we found an oppression so great as to make life unbearable. Murder is common, youths and women flogged, imprisoned without trial, arrested without reason, theft of personal property under name of requisition. Condition of affairs prevails difficult for Western European to realize who has not seen and heard the evidence. People are forced to take an oath of allegiance to Rumanian King; if they refuse, they are persecuted. Experienced Hungarian Directors of Hospitals have been replaced by inexperienced Rumanian doctors. Rumanian military authorities demand petition for every passport, request for coal or food. Petition must be written in Rumanian language, Rumanian lawyer must be employed, and he charges enormous fees ... Last Good Friday Rumanians advanced suddenly to Boros-Sebes and two hundred and fifty Hungarian soldiers were taken prisoners. These were killed in most barbarous manner; stripped naked and stabbed with bayonets in way to prolong life as long as possible.*

Milk was stolen regularly from railroad cars; officers and soldiers of the army of occupation frequently made excursions to the city markets and grabbed the merchandise from the tables without paying for it. On September 19th, an abortive attempt was made to pillage the National Museum, upon the pretext that about one hundred boxes of materials were transferred to Budapest from Transylvania by Hungarian authorities, and they belonged to Rumania. The plan failed because Allied officers led by U. S. General Bandholtz stood at the door of the building when the vans and soldiers arrived. Later most of the Transylvanian rarities had to be given to the Rumanians as the result of an order of the Peace

Conference, well before the peace treaty sanctioned the occupation of East Hungary.

During the months of the Rumanian rule, trains carried to the Regat (Old Rumania) the booty that was collected in factories, offices, and private apartments. The railroad cars were never returned. Telephone sets were ripped from the walls; horses and hay were confiscated from foreign citizens also, as Bulgarian Consul General Neicoff reported to Romanelli. Common criminals were freed from police prisons if they had influential friends among Rumanian officers.

The Peace Conference was infuriated. A telegram sent by the Supreme Council to the Rumanian government on August 14th called attention to "the directions forwarded on three occasions by the Conference to the Mission of Allied Generals and communicated to Budapest." Among these were disarmament of the Hungarian troops, maintenance of order with a minimum of foreign troops, provisioning of Hungary, abstention from all interference with internal politics, and the allowing of the free expression of the national will. The Supreme Council insisted that "no definite recovery of war material, railroad material, agricultural supplies, or stock, etc., may take place at the present time."

The Allies were not enthusiastic about their turncoat friend, who until 1916 belonged to the camp of the Central Powers. General Bliss angrily criticized the Rumanian government at a secret meeting held in the Villa Majestic on July 17th, because the Rumanian army repeatedly crossed the demarcation line in Hungary and was unwilling to withdraw. The occupation of Budapest added fuel to the fire. As Viscount Bryce explained in the House of Lords on December 16th, 1919, the conduct of the Rumanian troops was "anything but creditable," and "it called for the attention of the Allied Powers, who were obliged to remonstrate with them on the way they were behaving."[66]

The Allies finally agreed to negotiations which started in the Vienna office of Colonel Cuninghame. General Gorton and the British Consul also participated at the meeting, together with Count Bethlen, the head of the Anti-Bolshevist Committee and Böhm, the diplomatic representative of the Budapest government.

Cuninghame made an introductory statement, emphasizing that the Entente was not in a position to recognize two Hungarian governments, and neither of them would be recognized until the inclusion of representatives of different elements of the political spectrum. He suggested that every social class must have representation and the two governments should make a compromise in order to remove the Rumanians from the country.

Bethlen suggested the formation of a new government in which the bourgeois group, the farmers and the workers would each get one third of the portfolios. Böhm declared that the proposal was unacceptable. Then Gorton said that the Peidl government should be supplemented by two members of the Szeged government. Böhm's reaction was positive to the idea, but Bethlen didn't like it. Finally they all agreed that General Gorton would go to Budapest, the Szeged government would hold back its troops in order to avoid bloodshed, the two Hungarian governments would be informed about the negotiations, and that they would convene again within three days. At the next meeting a representative of the Szeged government, the Italian Prince Borghese and the emissary of the French government, H. Alizé will be present, according to the agreement. Apparently the lifting of the blockade was the result of the first meeting. As it turned out, it didn't solve any other problems.

Comunication between Budapest and Paris was slow; Romanelli did not receive any instructions, and the organization of the anti-Peidl civilian and military elements progressed rapidly in the first days of August. In smaller Hungarian towns the first news of the resignation of the Soviet government was interpreted as the sign for the expulsion of the local Communists from their posts. In Zalaegerszeg national flags decorated the streets in the morning of August 2. The commander of the Red Guard, József Bátori himself gave orders for the removal of red stars and other symbols. In a few days the exponents of the Soviet government disappeared from offices and streets. The campaigns of anti-communist elements discouraged the moderates in the workers' movement many of whom supported Peidl. Everybody with connections to the fallen regime was under suspicion. An Action Committee of Budapest civil employees sent a delegation to Peidl on August 5th and demanded the firing of the former Commissars. Peidl remarked that he wanted to leave out the "red exponents" from his cabinet, too, but asked for time. It seemed to the delegation that the head of the government wanted to dodge the issue. The opposition called the rule of the Peidl cabinet "masked proletarian dictatorship" from the day of its creation.

On August 6th the police and some army units were already controlled by the conspirators. In the afternoon, they arrested Interior Minister Peyer for a short while and learned from him that the Council of Ministers was holding a meeting in the Sándor Palace, near the Royal Castle in Buda. As a result the original plan that required the arrest of the ministers in the ministries was dropped. General Schnetzer and his men, under the protection of the Rumanian army, occupied the Ministry of Defense without resistance. At the same time Dr. Csilléry, who represented Archduke Joseph and the counter-revolutionary "White House" organization, went to the Sándor Palace with forty mounted policemen and some army officers.[67]

Inside the palace the Council of Ministers was in session. The first item on the agenda was the report of Foreign Minister Ágoston on the armistice negotiations. The government approved the text of a note that was supposed to be sent to the Rumanians. The ministers later discussed Clemenceau's radio-telegram. The French Premier promised in it that he would send four Entente generals to Budapest instead of troops. Peidl indignantly informed his colleagues that

61

the Rumanian censor vetoed the publication of the telegram in Hungarian newspapers.

Haubrich, the Minister of Defense, was the next speaker. He submitted the draft of a government decree about the disarmament of the Hungarian Red Army, "which became necessary in view of the new situation." The draft was accepted.

Prime Minister Peidl started to discuss the problem of an expense-forecast for the Armistice Committee, when the door opened and an official reported to him that police and army units had occupied the building, locked the doors, and ordered everyone to stay in the palace until further notice.[88]

Accompanied by policemen and army officers, Csilléry soon entered the room holding a walking stick in his hand and demanded the resignation of the government in the name of the "United Revolutionary Parties." He informed Peidl that the cabinet would be arrested if he disobeyed the order.

Peidl mildly protested and stated that he had resigned when Kun took over, because he disagreed with the communist dictatorship and opposed any new attempt to establish an authoritarian regime. After emphasizing that he had received his appointment from the Workers' Council and could return it to that body only, he assured Csilléry that "in the interest of social peace" he was considering the formation of a provisional coalition government "with the participation of the Social Democrats" just before the meeting of the Council of Ministers, and asked the uninvited uniformed visitors to leave the room.

In the meantime General Schnetzer arrived from the Ministry of Defense and told Peidl and the ministers that he would take personal responsibility for their safety. He also promised that if the government resigned, the ministries would be taken over by those who are second in rank and in a few months a new coalition government would be formed with the participation of the middle class, peasantry, and the workers.

Following a short debate that took place in the absence of the conspirators, the government decided to yield to force and resign. Peidl repeated that the resignation took place under compulsion, remarked that the Rumanian army, which backed the coup d'etat, had arrested several innocent workers and other Hungarians, and raised the question of responsibility for the overthrow of the government.

The minutes of the cabinet meeting prove that Peidl and his associates did not put up a stout resistance. The Prime Minister must have felt that his caretaker government was doomed to failure. He knew that under the premiership of a former parliamentary representative, D. Ábrahám Pattantyus, a new counter-revolutionary government was formed in Szeged on July 12th, and there were thus two Hungarian governments in existence, both with their hands tied.[99] In addition to them, the Anti-Bolshevist Committee in Vienna also vindicated the power. It is entirely possible that Peidl lost his faith in a satisfactory settlement and wanted to get rid of his responsibilities anyhow.

Foreign Minister Ágoston called Böhm in Vienna and asked for Allied intervention, but nothing happened. Prince Borghese advised Böhm next morning that he had to contact Count Bethlen, the head of the Anti-Bolshevist Committee.

On August 6th King Ferdinand of Rumania was already on his way to Budapest. He arrived there on August 7th to add to the humiliation of the Hungarians.

The consequences of the violent removal of the Peidl government were tragic in Hungarian internal politics as well as in foreign affairs. It made impossible any kind of sincere cooperation between the Social Democrats and the conservative forces and alienated many decent politicians who disliked unlawful methods and foreign interference. It was impossible to tame and transform the Hungarian Soviet regime into a People's Republic again, since it had been overthrown once, was not popular any more and the attempt was doomed to failure from the beginning. Yet it is also true that the nation needed a peaceful transitionary period during which passions could be calmed and the spirit of reconciliation could prevent rush actions. After four centuries of Habsburg rule, the majority of the nation was watching the royalist counter-revolutionary takeover with mixed feelings.

The coup d'etat was also a blow to Hungarian hopes in the international arena. In Paris the representatives of the Successor States could frighten benevolent delegates again with the monster of Habsburg restoration.[70] On the other hand, Habsburg rule in Austria-Hungary was over and the Peace Conference didn't want to put Charles back on his throne.[71] Benes was not sure of it for a while and repeatedly said at meetings of the Peace Conference that "the Magyars did not admit their defeat. They remained imperialist in spirit... There were strong objections to the course of negotiating with any Hungarian Party." Habsburg restoration in any part of the former Monarchy could have meant reunification, which was highly undesirable for the governments of those countries which gained or regained independence.

VII. ADMIRAL HORTHY TAKES OVER

As the result of the successful "Putsch," Archduke Joseph became Regent, and he in turn appointed István Friedrich Prime Minister. Schnetzer received the Defense portfolio.[72] Joseph and Friedrich hurriedly called on General Gorton, Admiral Troubridge and Colonel Romanelli and reported to them that they took over the government. Now the Paris Peace Conference was confronted with three problems: "The looting by the Rumanian army, the return of the Habsburgs to power, and food supply."[73] The "Big Four" asked the Rumanians on August 7th "if they intended to defy the Allies," but the invaders were unwilling to submit to the demands. Bucharest was encouraged by French army leaders, whose support meant more than the official warnings. They remained in Budapest and extended the occupation zone to Transdanubia.

According to the minutes of a meeting of the Interallied

Military Mission in Budapest, "there was a possibility of the Entente's accepting Friedrich's government,"[74] which probably included the recognition of the regency. Friedrich made preparations for a long office term; his cabinet issued several decrees in a row. The first one returned to landowners large estates which were nationalized by the Soviets. The ardour of Friedrich was dampened by only one thing: the National Army, which was organized by Admiral Horthy in French-occupied Szeged, grew into a formidable force, but the Rumanians did not allow Friedrich to establish another one. The leaders of the Entente Missions explained to him that they did not have a military force which could protect the new government.

Friedrich had to look for support elsewhere. Gusztáv Gratz, the new Hungarian envoy in Vienna, visited Chancellor Renner in October, 1919 and asked him to accept the idea of a Polish-Hungarian-Austrian block which was originally proposed by the Polish government. The plan proved abortive, and Friedrich realized that there was only one way open: he recommended that Joseph confirm Horthy's appointment as Commander-in-Chief. The Szeged government that was reorganized by Dezső Pattantyus Ábrahám on July 12th included some liberals, and those whom the Allies considered rightists — such as Horthy and Captain Gömbös — were left out, although the Admiral retained his Commander-in-Chief position. The Allies showed more willingness to negotiate with the new Szeged regime; Horthy's recruiting attempts were hindered less often. The anti-communist Serbian government was the only one which accredited a diplomatic representative of the counter-revolutionary group, following a trip to Belgrade by Horthy and Count Teleki of the Anti-Bolshevist Committee. This was important because the National Army had to cross Serbian-occupied territory to reach Western Hungary, and this was impossible without the approval of Prime Minister Protic' government.

Horthy realized that he could lean on the power of bayonets and demanded Prime Minister Ábrahám to make his command independent of the Ministry of War. His troops were soon on the march to the unoccupied sector of Western Hungary and didn't pay any attention to the order of the Interallied Military Mission which demanded that the troops had to be withdrawn to Szeged. Horthy himself flew from Szeged, leaving the French in the belief that he was going to drop the return order over his troops. Instead of this, he landed in Siófok at the Lake Balaton. Two days later the vanguard of his army arrived there and continued its march to the North. The National Army controlled part of Hungary; Horthy was in a position to initiate negotiations with the Allies.

The Commander-in-Chief of the National Army was fifty years old then, well beyond the age when most political and military leaders climb to the top. He was born in the village on Kenderes in Central Hungary, the fifth child of landowner István Horthy. At the age of 14 he entered the Naval Academy of the Monarchy, and graduated on October 1st, 1886. After that, for decades he seldom visited Hungary and his Hungarian became rusty, because German was the language of command in the Navy.[75]

As a naval officer, he saw a large part of the world. In 1908 Horthy became the commander of the warship Taurus which was stationed in Constantinople, to provide protection in that troubled city for the personnel of the Austro-Hungarian legation. One year later the newly promoted Corvette Captain received a great honor; he was ordered to Vienna to serve as one of Francis Joseph's four aide-de-camps. His service was most likely outstanding, because in the spring of 1914 when he was released from the Court, Horthy got the title of Chamberlain and a purebred horse in addition to another promotion.

During the war, the advancement of professional officers was much faster than in peace times. The fleet of the Monarchy was a prisoner of the narrow Adriatic Sea most of the time, but Horthy, as the commander of the fast ship Novara, broke out from the enemy ring successfully in May 1917. In February 1918, Horthy was invited to the headquarters of

Charles, the new ruler, who named him Commander of the Fleet, which meant that he was promoted over the head of many of his comrades. According to the 1917 edition of the *Almanach für die k. und k. Kriegsmarine* Horthy was 24th in line among 46 "Linienschiffkapitaene." Charles apparently wanted to reward the loyalty and faithful service of the former aide-de-camp, hoping that firm and determined leadership might rescue his navy from disintegration. The successful suppression of the mutiny at the Cattaro naval base in February, 1918 proved that Horthy was determined to represent the interests of his warlord, but it was too late then; the war was almost over. On October 31st, Charles ordered Horthy to transfer his ships to the South Slav National Council.

A splendid naval career ended. Horthy returned to Kenderes and was busy with farming until a messenger of Count Gyula Károlyi arrived from Szeged with the request that he should take over the Ministry of War in the counter-revolutionary government. At almost the same time, Count Bethlen of the Vienna Anti-Bolshevist Committee made a similar proposition to him. After some thinking, Horthy sided with the Szeged organization, believing that the French-occupied Hungarian city was a better jumping board than Vienna, which most Hungarians associated with Habsburg rule.

The Allies changed their mind upon Czech pressure and forced Archduke Joseph to resign from the regency on August 23rd, 1919. On that day, an emissary of the Peace Conference, Sir George Clerk, arrived in Hungary to promote the formation of a democratic regime which would be acceptable to the Allies. The negotiations took place in Clerk's Budapest apartment. On November 5th, Horthy met there with Vázsonyi, the leader of the National Democratic Bourgeois Party, Nagyatádi Szabó of the Smallholders' Party, Garami, who represented the Social Democratic Party, and National Party leader Lovászy. Horthy denied that the occupation of the capital city by the National Army would result in a military dictatorship, and officially declared that he stood on the basis of civil rights, remarking that his army would eradicate every form of Bolshevism. His attitude soothed the doubts of Clerk and the party leaders, who all knew that resentments of the conservatives and revenge-seeking sentiments erupted into violence in different areas of the country. Bands of army officers handed out punishment indiscriminately to those who in their opinion were associated with the Kun and Károlyi regimes. Many of the officers were of Austro-German extraction, others got their military training in the army of Francis Joseph, where German was the official language, and it was easy to be converted in thinking and behavior into a mixture of Austrian and Hungarian. The old Hungarian virtue of nonchalant broad-mindedness was missing from them.

In August and September, hundreds of suspected Communists were hanged or otherwise executed without trial.[76] The foreign echo of the murders was very unfavorable, and Horthy wanted to stop illegal actions after a while, but the ghost could not be put back into the bottle easily.[77] The fury of the officers turned frequently against Jewish radicals who had formed "almost the whole of Károlyi's intellectual General Staff, and nearly all Béla Kun's Commissaries, including the most notorious perpetrators of the Red Terror which had preceded the White; although, even so, many of the most violent White Terrorists would have denied that they were attacking Jews as such."[78] The eradication of Bolshevism was their admitted goal. To endow the appearance of legality, concentration camps were organized for politically dangerous elements. Finally a cabinet decree was published in the official *Budapest Gazette* on June 13, 1920 according to which the dissolution of special military organizations became necessary "for the tranquilazation of aroused public opinion." It emphasized that the investigative activities of the commandos ceased, and the police along with the gendarmery took over such functions. An editorial in the November 19th issue of the daily *Az Est* pointed out that return to productive labor and "establishing peace with ourselves and the whole world" could be the solution. A headline in the same issue indicated that according to a government decree "stores should be closed at 4, offices at 3 p.m. Only one light bulb can be used in each room."

Horthy's entry into Budapest at the head of his troops on November 16, 1919 meant the return of traditionalist forces. In his reply to the speech of the Mayor, Horthy criticized the capital city which "has disowned her thousand years of tradition, dragged the Holy Crown and the national colours in the dust, and clothed herself in red rags. The finest of the nation she threw into dungeons and drove into exile. She laid in ruin our property and wasted our wealth." The Admiral could have mentioned the senseless and disastrous war among the causes of Hungarian problems, but he remained silent about it. After thirty-two years in uniform, he could not get that far, but declared that he was ready to forgive Budapest "if she will turn from her false gods to the service of the Fatherland." Those politicians who had sensitive ears, understood that Horthy was in charge and gathered around the new source of power.[79]

Friedrich was regarded in Allied circles as a representative of feudalist interests. His government was never recognized officially; he had to go. On November 23rd, Károly Huszár took over the premiership from Friedrich, who also lacked Horthy's confidence because of his erratic behavior during the months of the Károlyi regime. Friedrich's unlimited ambitions stood in the way of the Supreme Commander, who wanted to secure the power for himself, at least temporarily.

Huszár was a grade school teacher by profession, without any experience in policy making, but he was acceptable for the Entente. His government was formed from representatives of the Party of Christian National Unity, the National Liberal Party, the Smallholders' Party, the Agrarian Party, the International Social Democratic Party, and the Democratic Party. Independent-royalist Count Sommsich became the Foreign Minister, and Friedrich received the Ministry of War, which was insignifcant because the army accepted orders from Horthy only.

The participation of the Social Democratic party in the coalition government did not mean that it had changed course since the Friedrich coup d'etat. Those moderate party leaders who did not escape from Hungary simply wanted to find a temporary *modus vivendi* with the bourgeois and peasant political forces, believing that it would have a moderating effect on the counter-revolutionaries and that the country was in such a desperate position that sincere cooperation even with the devil was necessary. On December 18th, the leaders of the party instructed Minister of Labor and Public Welfare Peyer and Vice Minister of Commerce Miákits to resign, but chang· ed their mind two days later "in view of the foreign political situation." Finally, after several political trials, electoral irregularities, and the destruction of the printing presses of the party newspaper, Peyer and Miákits left the cabinet on January 15th, 1920.

On December 2nd, 1919 Huszár received the invitation of the Peace Conference, and on January 25-27, 1920 members of the National Assembly were elected in Budapest, Transdanubia and in the area between the rivers Danube and Tisza, from which the Rumanian troops were withdrawn. Nagyatádi Szabó's Smallholders' Party received 79 seats, the Party of Christian National Unity got 75, the Democratic Party 6. Four independents were also elected. The Smallholders' Party representatives were in majority anti-Habsburg; the Christian Unity party had royalist tendencies. It was evident that things would come to a crisis, sooner or later.

The Supreme Commander himself created the impression during conversations with supporters of Charles that his restoration would be very difficult if not impossible, because "he has so many enemies here." It is, of course, understandable that the Hungarians, most of whom lived in poverty after the war and were confused by ever-changing extremist ideologies, could not care less about the future form of state. Constitutional problems were not considered significant by most people.

Meanwhile, the supporters of Horthy and the nationalist,

70

anti-Habsburg organizations worked hard to convince the nation that a head of state had to be elected, before the conclusion of the peace treaty. The chief of the Intelligence Section of the National Army instructed the political officers to spread the news that "there was a man who had the ability to lead the country, and that was Miklós Horthy." Telegrams from mass meetings demanded Horthy's election, and the office of the Comander-in-Chief had to be informed about the drafting of the law which was supposed to fill the gap in the supreme national leadership.

The National Assembly started to discuss the law on February 26th, and after just a few days on March 1st, it was ready to elect a Regent. Admiral Horthy received 131 votes from 141. Liberal Count Albert Apponyi got 7 votes; Joseph Habsburg was not even considered, because of the resistance of the Peace Conference and the Successor States.

During the elections, the Parliament building was surrounded by officers. Some of Apponyi's supporters were not allowed to enter the building, and one Minister, Baron Frigyes Korányi, was also stopped at the door,[80] but is is undeniable that the 131 votes represented an absolute majority in the 160 member Assembly. The voting was secret; on the other hand, the presence of the military was a serious legal defect. As a parliamentary committee report stated, "when the Regent arrived at the Parliament, a large number of soldiers wearing service insignia and equipped with weapons, partly with hand grenades, invaded the building without permission. Many of the soldiers appeared in the great hall before the oath was taken; during the oath, they blocked the entrance doors and didn't let the members of the Assembly enter from the corridors. Armed guards and sentries also could be seen in other parts of the Parliament building. The said armed gathering obstructed the National Assembly in the free exercise of its occupation."

This was a clear and courageous statement, but the conclusion was compromising: "In view of the fact that the President of the House issued a firm declaration on the 2nd

71

day of this month and enforced the authority of the National Assembly, it is recommended that the grievance be considered void." The representatives surrendered to the military; Horthy did not have a rival at home. Only the problem of royal power remained unsettled. The shadow of the physically frail and mentally soft Habsburg King stretched over the country.

VIII. THE TRIANON PEACE TREATY

Most Hungarians realized that further resistance was in vain, and it would only prolong the period of uncertainty, when the much stronger Germany signed the peace treaty in Versailles on June 28th, 1919, and Austria signed the Treaty of Neuilly three months later. Former Prime Minister Friedrich was one of those who opposed the peace negotiations, believing that the Successor States would rapidly crumble and fall apart; therefore, Hungary had to wait patiently and assume for a while the role of an international outcast. Regent Horthy and Premier Huszár wanted to conclude the peace treaty for different reasons. Horthy wanted to strengthen his rule and create political stability. Huszár was convinced that the peace treaty was inevitable and Hungarians could not be kept in doubt any longer.

On January 16th the Allies presented the peace conditions to the Hungarian delegation in Paris. The Peace Conference approved the Treaty on February 26, 1919, but it was delivered to the Hungarian peace delegation almost one year later. The peace-makers in Paris accepted the view that the principle of self-determination called for the separation from Hungary of all non-Magyars, and passed by geographical and economic problems.

The reply of the Huszár government was delivered on February 10th. It denied that the Slovaks, Rumanians, Croatians and smaller nationalities intended to join the Czechs, Old (Regat) Rumanians and the Serbs; it also disputed the claims that the nationalities constituted a majority in all the areas to be detached, and asked for plebiscites. As could be expected, the Hungarian proposal was rejected on May 6th, and the draft of the treaty was declared final. Premier Huszár didn't want to share the responsibility for the treaty and resigned on March 14th.[81] Sándor Simonyi-Semadám, the Deputy Speaker of the National Assembly, became the new Prime Minister on March 15th.

Count Apponyi, a well known royalist and liberal politician, was the leader of the Hungarian peace delegation. He delivered a speech before the Peace Conference listing statistical, geopolitical and economic data in three languages, but the only result of his reasoning was Lloyd George's remark: "I hope that he will not make another speech in Japanese..." President Wilson's sublime ideas about "justice and equality of right" and about the nations of the world being entitled "not only to free pathways upon the sea but also to assured and unmolested access to those pathways" were completely forgotten. Clemenceau, Lloyd George and others also did not pay any attention to another Wilsonian promise "not to... impair or rearrange the Austro-Hungarian Empire."[82] As it turned out, Germany's territorial losses were not even comparable to those suffered by Austria and Hungary, although that country also had sizeable national and linguistic minorities.

On June 4th the Hungarian peace treaty was signed in the Trianon Palace at Versailles. From the 325,000 sq. km. which comprised the area of Hungary, only 92,963 sq. km. was left. Rumania had received 103,093; Czechoslovakia 61,633; Yugoslavia's territory increased by 63,092 sq. km. Smaller chunks were given to Austria, Poland and Italy. Of the 9,945,000 persons of Magyar tongue,[83] more than 3,000,000 found themselves in the Successor States.

As one of the most competent experts, Oszkár Jászi, wrote "in order that some 1,700,000 Slovaks might be freed, 1,000,000 Magyars and 260,000 Germans are now exiled from their homeland; in order that 3,000,000 Rumanians might be incorporated into Greater Rumania, about 1,700,000 Magyars

This map was drawn by the representatives of Czech, Slovak, Polish, Ukrainian, Lithuanian, and Rumanian emigré organizations at a meeting held in Independence Hall, Philadelphia and published by the American press on October 28, 1918. It contains almost every element of the post World War I European territorial rearrangement, including the new boundaries of Hungary and the Danzig corridor. The armistice between the Allies and Austria-Hungary was concluded on November 3, 1918. Hungary had to sign the peace treaty on June 4, 1920. Thus the fate of the country was obviously sealed before the start of the peace negotiations.

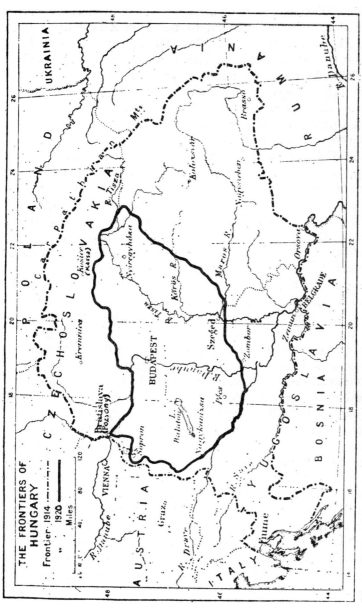

THE FRONTIERS OF
HUNGARY
Frontier 1914 ....
1920 ———

More than 3,000,000 Magyars, many of them living in immediate juxtaposition to the frontier, were separated from Hungary by the treaty of Trianon. The country lost 71.4 per cent of its territory and 61 per cent of its population.

and 600,000 Germans have been separated from Hungary; in order that 500,000 Serbs might build up a new State with their racial kindred, about 400,000 Magyars and 300,000 Germans have been forced into a new allegiance; in order that 250,000 Germans might return to their racial home, about 50,000 Magyars and a like number of Croats have had to share their fate. In round number, 5,500,000 souls were liberated from the old irredenta, at the price of plunging 4,500,000 into a new one."

A British expert of Hungarian affairs stated that "it was not genuine self-determination that was applied at all, but a sort of national determinism which assumed that all peoples in Hungary of the same or kindred stock as their neighbours ought to be transferred; their wishes were taken for granted. Thus the Ruthenes of the north-east were attached to Czechoslovakia, although they were neither Czechs nor Slovaks, simply because they they were not Magyars."[84]

The treaty did not pay any attention to interrelationship between agricultural and industrial areas, split railroad lines and even cities. It required Hungary to pay an unspecified sum in reparations, which was to be "the first charge upon all her assets and resources," prohibited the draft for military service and limited the Hungarian armed forces to 35,000 professional mercenaries, to be used only for the maintenance of order and frontier defense.

Hungary lost all its gold, silver, mercury, copper, and salt mines, almost one-half of its coal fields, and all but one of its iron mines. More than four-fifths of its forests were also given to the Successor States. Following the peace treaty the formerly largely self-supporting country had to import most of the raw materials for its industry that grew considerably during the war years and provided livelihood for 25% of Hungarians. Budapest — which was designed for pre-Trianon Hungary — became a hydrocephalic capital city. Industrial, cultural and human resources were all concentrated there after the loss of factories and mining areas, universities, museums and libraries.

Trianon included provisions which were hardly justified by any consideration. Prohibiting the production of heavy artillery, tanks and military airplanes, it also banned the manufacturing of civilian aircraft. Among the categories of indemnification, the cost of the anti-Soviet war expenses came first; thereby the Allies repeated the method which was used against the Károlyi regime, not concerning themselves with the politically and ideologically different new government but making it responsible for the acts of the imperial government, too.

Enemy occupation of Hungarian territory forced more than 400,000 Hungarians to escape. Many of them settled in Budapest and other cities, living in railroad cars and slums. It was the result of such circumstances that "there began in Europe a great and exciting drama: the fight for the revision of the Versailles Peace. It was one of the greatest and most dramatic struggles in the political history of Europe. It ended in a new tragedy, vast and destructive: the second World War," as Edward Benes wrote in his *Memoirs*. Benes also emphasized that the struggle for revision "was a normal development" in a certain sense, because after every war the defeated party tries to wipe out its defeat, "either by political or diplomatic means, or by a new war." But it was not only the defeated who turned against the victors. The reshaping of Central Europe brought other results, too. Nationalism became a dominant force among Slovaks, Macedonians, Croatians and others, who turned against their new masters seeking complete independence. The Hungarian press started to complain about the oppression of Hungarian minorities in Rumania, Czechoslovakia and Yugoslavia. In Rumanian Transylvania, German (Saxon) and Hungarian minorities frequently referred to past independence of the area, during which Calvinist, Catholic, Greek Orthodox and Unitarian churches enjoyed complete religious freedom and there was only a minimum of friction among the major nationalities.

The treaty was clearly punitive.[85] Data in percentages show how difficult it was to even attempt reconstruction. Hungary could keep only 28.6 per cent of her former territory; 31.3 per cent was given to Rumania, 19.6 per cent to Yugoslavia, 18.9 per cent to Czechoslovakia; 1.2 per cent (Burgenland) was awarded to Austria. Poland and Italy received smaller fragments. France, the dominant continental power in postwar Europe, hoped that she could rely on the Successor States and didn't worry about Hungary's fate.

The problem of responsibility for the Treaty has haunted Hungarian politicians ever since 1920. The Social Democratic daily *Népszava* said in an editorial on June 21, 1928: "A forgery of historical facts is going on. The regime would like to shift the responsibility for the destruction, collapse and dissection of Hungary to those men and parties who attempted to save what could be saved of the ruined country. Shameless falsifiers shout from certain political circles that the war could be won if October [of 1918] wouldn't have come..." Although the representatives of the Horthy regime signed the Treaty under coercion, it cannot be denied that Károlyi and Kun both fought for a while for the territorial integrity of Hungary, risking their political existence instead of giving in. Károlyi's pacifism and the internationalist attitudes of the Republic of Councils cannot wash away the fact that they also represented the ideology of Hungarian irredenta, long before Admiral Horthy consolidated his power.

As it turned out, Czechoslovakia, Rumania and Yugoslavia did not eliminate the errors of Hungarian nationality policy, but frequently added to them. "The Trianon peace treaty did not mean the democratic solution of the nationality problem. It healed old wounds by inflicting new ones, and did not put an end to the hostility and animosity that existed between the peoples of the Danube Valley, but increased them among new conditions."[86]

IX. HABSBURG RESTORATION ATTEMPTS

Charles renounced participation in the affairs of the state and recognized the decision in regard to the future form of state of Hungary in advance on November 13th, 1918. It is undeniable that he opened the way toward the establishment of the People's Republic and legalized the actions of the Károlyi government as well as of the Hungarian Soviet Republic, but he did not resign the throne. When his advisers thought that the time was ripe for action in Hungary, Charles and especially the ambitious Queen Zita started to make plans for a return.

According to a confidential report of the Hungarian police, "throughout the winter of 1921, His Majesty was surrounded by a peculiar mixture of people who represented opposing political views and whose role could not be entirely clarified." A Captain Werkman was one of the King's chief advisers. Werkman's sister-in-law, who divorced her physician husband and became a movie actress under the name of Fifi Cantora, lived together in Salzburg with Bolgyai, another Hungarian, who was deported earlier from Switzerland because of alleged spy activities.

In November and December 1920, Mrs. Werkman, Miss Cantora, and Baroness Eimann spent several days together in Bern, apparently discussing plans for the return of Charles to Hungary. During that period, Miss Cantora met an international adventurer who carried a Spanish passport, had close connections with Bolgyai and conferred sometimes with German communist leader Levi. Later the Swiss police confiscated the letters which Miss Cantora received from Erzberger, a German pacifist politician. The content of the correspondence was not made public.

As it turned out, the Chateau of Prangins, bordering the Lake Geneva, was an excellent place for secret talks. An old bachelor who owned a house on the Lausanne-Prangins road rented rooms to friends of the King. He could leave through a back door, walk some hundred yards through the vineyards, and inside the villa meetings could be held with supporters — sometimes without the knowledge of the detectives and newspapermen who constantly watched Charles' movements.

In January 1921, Dr. János Török (Toch), "the former field priest of Count Mihály Károlyi," visited Charles. The police report stated that Dr. Török was a spy of the Italian and French governments during the war, and the Károlyi revolution freed him from the Star Prison of Szeged.[87]

A high ranking Swiss police officer whose name had been omitted from the report told the Hungarian agents that "they were suspicious for a long time of the many different people who were loafing around the King." He had the impression that "His Majesty was under constant surveillance, especially on the part of the Socialists and Communists." This was a clear implication that Charles was sympathetic to the liberal-leftist cause and wanted to reestablish a Károlyi-type regime, if not worse, in Hungary.

It belongs to the antecedents that after his election Regent Horthy sent a letter to the King, assuring him that the Regency was provisional, and he was eager to return the power to the crowned ruler as soon as circumstances would permit. Charles was under the impression that Horthy served as his proconsul, for two reasons. First, the Kingdom of Hungary was restored, and the law that created the regency contained no provision for a successor.[88] Second, the repeated loyalty declarations of the new head of the Hungarian state seemed to prove that he was making preparations for the return of the King.[89] Horthy at that time was under the influence of royalist politicians such as Counts Andrássy, Sigray, Pallavicini, the influential Speaker of the National Assembly István Rakovszky, and foreign expert Gratz.[90] It is very likely though, that some members of the royal household observed the shadowing attempts of Horthy's political police, and this must have given impetus to the rushing of the trip. It is possible that another factor was also considered by Charles and Zita. In connection with the coup d'etat of István Friedrich, there were rumors that Hungarian monarchist circles considered a number of foreign and domestic personalities for the throne. Beside Archduke Joseph the names of the Duke of Connaught, Italian Prinze d'Abruzzi, Crown Prince Charles of Rumania, and Prince Cyril, the son of the former Czar of Bulgaria were mentioned. Crown Prince Ottó, the son of Charles, also had supporters who wanted him to rule after a period of tutoring as a constitutional monarch. On November 19 the world press reported that the Queen of Rumania visited ex-ruler Charles and offered him a large amount of money to renounce claims to the Hungarian throne in order to bring about consolidation in the country and unite Rumania and Hungary under the Rumanian crown.

There were other offers, too. In early 1919 representatives of the Austrian, Czechoslovak, Polish and South-Slav governments visited Charles to discuss with him the material indemnification for the confiscated property of the royal family. The wealth of the former ruler was partly invested in stocks and shares in industrial companies; castles and huge land holdings made up the other part. The Successor States wanted to obtain loans from banks of neutral countries offering these holdings as security.

The negotiations took place in Zürich. The Emperor was offered the sum of 184 million Swiss francs, payable in four years. In return he was supposed to promise not to set foot for twenty-five years in any state that was formerly part of the Dual Monarchy and to reliquish all claims to the throne on behalf of himself and his heirs.

Charles politely but firmly declined, explaining that his sovereign claims can be settled in association with his peoples. "Should these call me, I shall return," he said.

István Werbőczy's *Tripartite,* written early in the 16th century and considered for centuries the best expression of Hungarian constitutional law, clearly stated that the royal rights of the kings were the property of the nation, which transferred them to the ruler with the symbol of the Holy Crown of Stephen I. Throughout Hungarian history the nation (i.e. the nobility) reserved this right. Although the

Pragmatic Sanction temporarily suspended it, the law was still in force in the case of vacancy of the throne or if royal power could not be exercised for any serious reason, as Public Law I of 1910 explained it. Charles did not resign but escaped from the territory of the Dual Monarchy, did not exercise his royal powers for one and a half years, and recognized in advance Hungary's future form of state. On the other hand much was at stake, and the situation changed basically when the communist regime collapsed and loyalist forces seemed to grab the power in one of his former countries.

The Paris Peace Conference considered the Habsburg question on February 2, 1920. In a note that the Allied and Associated Powers sent to the Hungarian Peace Delegation in Neuilly, they denied the rumors which, misleading public opinion, "made them appear to recognize and help the return of the Habsburg dynasty to the Hungarian throne." The Allies were convinced that the restoration of a dynasty which represented the oppression of foreign nationalities in the view of its subjects would not be compatible with the ideas for which the war was fought and the liberation of the suppressed people. The note emphasized that a Habsburg restoration would "neither be recognized nor tolerated," and the Allies would not consider it an internal affair of Hungary.

This was a clear warning which could not be misunderstood. In Hungary, the position of the legitimist-royalist groups was made more difficult by the elections which gave a small majority to the anti-Habsburg Smallholders' Party. The copy of an anonymous letter found among the documents of Horthy, refers to a declaration that Charles was willing to make in order to bring the largest party over to the side of the "legitimate King." Count Hunyady, the Lord Steward of the royal household, drafted a declaration, the essence of which was that Charles was willing to share the supreme power with the nation, would recognize the independence of those states that were established on the ruins of the Dual Monarchy, and would take into consideration the political and legal status quo which developed in his absence.[91]

French policy in regard to restoration in Hungary was somewhat ambiguous. Prince Lajos Windischgraetz, one of Charles' emissaries to France, talked to Briand before the peace treaty was concluded. The French Foreign Minister believed that if Charles' return would not provoke the armed intervention of the Successor States, "a union of Hungary with Austria could prevent accession of the latter to Germany. That would render the tenure of Imperial authority in Central Europe not merely possible but even desirable. France could not of course officially support such a manifestly monarchical enterprise. All the same, entrenched once again on the banks of the Danube, the Habsburg crown would exercise its traditional attraction on the peoples of the Successor States which are themselves far from being firmly set in their mould."

Charles evidently knew that his return to the Hungarian throne was not advisable before the conclusion of the peace treaty, which was signed in June at the Trianon Palace in Versailles. The political and economic consequences of the treaty were grave. Areas which were part of the same country and people who lived under the same political roof for centuries could not be separated from each other without serious trouble. That was Hungary's problem, but members of the royal family had other ones in Switzerland. Members of Hungarian royalist organizations who frequently visited the King in Prangins reported at home that he had financial difficulties which contributed to his desire to regain power in Hungary. As a result of such news, Horthy informed Charles that his return to Hungary was entirely impossible under the given circumstances, but it was in vain. Charles decided to take over in Hungary.

His trip was well prepared. To divert suspicion, he often made excursions to distant places in Switzerland. His two pieces of luggage were sent ahead of him by Belgian Prince Sixtus of Parma, who assisted Charles during the war also, when he attempted to negotiate a peace settlement behind the back of the Germans. In the preparation of the trip, a Jacob

Larsen or Jack Lasques played a significant role. Lasques was traveling with a Spanish passport, which was accepted in post-war Europe without much questioning. In early March 1921, he reserved a seat in Paris both for Charles and himself for the Paris-Münich-Vienna express train. The trip was supposed to take place in three parts: the first one was the dangerous travel through Switzerland from Prangins to Basel. (As a political emigré, Charles was not allowed to leave the country.)

On March 24th, the King entered the train in Nyon, changed trains in Bern and crossed the border to Alsace-Lorraine with a simple border pass. Larsen-Lasques and a priest were accompanying him.

From Strassbourg he travelled with a Spanish passport that was secured for him in Paris and made out for a Senor Sanchez. German, Austrian, French and Czechoslovakian visas were stamped in it. In Salzburg, Austria, Lasques opened the door of the Pullman berth, showed the passport to the border guards and asked them not to wake up his companion, because he was ill and did not sleep all night. The second part of the trip ended in the palace of Count Erdődy in Vienna, where Charles had a long conversation with Lasques, who used the alias of Langues then.

In the morning of the 26th, Count Erdödy visited the Austrian passport office and another of the King's new companions, Prince Xavier, rented cars for the trip to Hungary.

Charles changed the color of his mustache from brown to black and wore a long travel coat and automobile glasses. The party arrived at the Hungarian border at 1 p.m. Charles and Erdődy continued the trip; Xavier returned to Vienna. The crossing of the Hungarian border was quite uneventful, except that the chauffeur did not have an international driver's license and tag and was only allowed to take his passengers to the border village of Pinkafő. From there Charles and Erdődy used a horse-drawn carriage and arrived at the Bishop's palace in Szombathely after 10 p.m. Next morning both of them left by car to Budapest.

Regent Horthy was having lunch when Major Magasházy, his aide-de-camp, entered with the message that Count Sigray, the Commissioner for Western Hungary, had an important message. Horthy was upset when the royalist Count reported to him that the King was waiting in the Prime Minister's residence and wanted to know whether Sigray was "in any way responsible" for the King's visit. According to Sigray's account neither he, nor Count Hunyady or any of the King's Hungarian confidants knew about his plans. The Regent told Sigray to go at once with his aide-de-camp to the Cabinet Chamber and "ask His Majesty to come to the Royal Palace." Horthy did not have to think very long of what he had to say to him. "This self-sought situation had only one solution: the King must return to Switzerland without delay."[92] The new ruler of Hungary recalled immediately his Székesfehérvár speech, in which he not only assured Charles of his loyalty, but also said that "before the restoration can be achieved, immense tasks of external and internal consolidation must be performed. Anyone who at present brings the question of the restoration of the monarchy to the fore will be doing a disservice to the peace of the country..." Legality supported Horthy's view, because the National Assembly declared itself the depository of the country's sovereignty in the second article of Public Law No. 1, and according to the 12th article the Regent was elected for the position of the head of state "until the National Assembly permanently settles the exercise of the supreme power."[93]

Charles wore a Hungarian officer's uniform when he entered the Regent's office. After embracing Horthy, he started to complain about life in exile. Horthy assured him that the royal estates had not been confiscated and the income deriving from them was at Charles' disposal, although "he asked the governments of the Successor States to contribute to the grant of His Majesty." The Admiral's statement contained promise as well as ambiguity, because if the Successor

States had given a negative answer, he was in a position to stop the Hungarian contribution.

To change the subject, Charles told Horthy that his return to Hungary had the blessing of France. The Regent replied that he had different information, and "the menace of a renewed occupation [of Hungary] was not imaginary."

At the end of the two-hour conversation, the King expressed his gratitude to Horthy and invested him with the Grand Cross of the Military Order of Maria Theresa — the highest military medal of the former Monarchy — and created him the Duke of Otranto and Szeged. Finally, the Regent asked his guest to retain his confidence in him and undertake nothing without consulting him first. Charles gave this account on the meeting: "Horthy received me at the Palace at the top of the stairs, stuttering that I was in grave peril. His embarrassment was painfully evident. I asked him to introduce his entourage, but he hustled me into his — formerly my — study. I talked to him for two hours, trying to achieve a practical working-basis. I wanted after all the lies and superfluous intrigues that there have been, to find a medium for future co-operation. There was no question of my resuming power right away," but issues of home and foreign policy had to be discussed. "Horthy kept on repeating that he held all the strings in his hand, that the country at large trusted only him, that I should try and sieze Vienna, and similar nonsense. Finally I asked him whether or not he proposed to adhere to our agreement. He replied that he rendered an oath to the National Assembly. 'In that case the simplest thing is for you to arrest me on the spot," I retorted, whereupon he became hysterical and I decided to go back to Szombathely."

"It was a bitterly cold evening and in the neighbourhood of Nagyvázsony our car broke down. I stood in the road for a long time until some peasant recognised and carried me to an inn. The Sunday night topers cheered me madly. I swallowed a hot grog, clasped fifty and more pairs of hands, and returned here with a raging temperature."

86

"I am glad to have cleared up at any rate the Horthy question and to have seen for myself that, apart from a small clique, everybody in Hungary is on my side."[94]

Charles was already on his way back to Szombathely, when Horthy called Fouchet, the French diplomatic representative, told him about the visit and requested him to ask Foreign Minister Briand whether the French government supported the return of Charles. The answer was an emphatic denial. Next day the Commissioners of England and France stressed the categorical opposition of their countries to such a step; later the Italian, Yugoslav, Czechoslovak and Rumanian governments also protested. The Yugoslavs and Czechoslovaks were ready to send an ultimatum demanding the departure of Charles, but he left Budapest in the meantime. On April 3rd the Entente Powers again demanded the expulsion of the King from Hungary. It seemed that the first post-war royal adventure was also the last, although Charles could not be chased away from Szombathely until April 5th.

On March 31st Hungary started a diplomatic counter-attack in Paris, basing it on Charles' statement about French promises. Hungarian chargé d'affaires Praznovszky visited the Quai d'Orsay and told Counselor Peretti that French political leaders encouraged the King. He pointed out that several public figures attended a meeting with Prince Sixtus of Parma, at which the topic was the planned return of Charles to Hungary. Peretti admitted that there were undisciplined politicians in Paris who flirted with such ideas, but they didn't represent the views of the government.

Horthy issued a General Order to the National Army on March 30th, thanked it for its loyalty, and declared that "a violent, sudden change in the government would threaten the existence of the nation." At that occasion, he omitted any reference to the future and did not even mention the King's name.

Meanwhile, Hungarian anti-Habsburg forces also went into action. Károly Hencz's April 1st resolution in the National Assembly stated that Charles' unexpected return endangered the existing legal order, and instructed the government to prevent any kind of subversive effort directed against the system established by the Regency law. Zoltán Meskó, another deputy, stressed in his speech that he had found "the great man of great times who is worthy of the name of the First Hungarian." His resolution expressed the deep gratitude and unswerving loyalty of Hungarians toward Horthy for his conduct during Charles' visit and said that the Regent "served the vital interests of the nation." The members of the Assembly stood up, applauded and sang the National Anthem. Royalist deputies were ducking; the King's cautious behavior discouraged them. Prime Minister Count Pál Teleki was the only one who bowed to his conscience and his critics; he didn't want to take sides between Charles and Horthy. Another reason for his resignation was that the Teleki cabinet included a number of legitimist ministers, who had to go.[95]

On April 14th Count István Bethlen formed the new government. The Transylvanian aristocrat supported conservative Count István Tisza until 1917; in 1919 he emigrated to Vienna and formed the Anti-Bolshevist Committee. After the fall of communism, Bethlen organized the Party of Christian National Unity.

The new Premier was a skilled politician, whose program included political and economic consolidation. One of his first acts was the removal of undesirable elements from the Regent's entourage. The hot-headed Prónay who was one of the organizers of the National Army and whose headquarters were established near the Royal Palace, Horthy's new residence, was sent home and his commando units were disbanded. Internal peace and quiet was more important than ever, because on April 23rd Rumania and Czechoslovakia, and on June 3rd Rumania and Yugoslavia signed a mutual military assistance pact that was directed against Hungary.

In the meantime, Charles' advisers believed that time was ripe for a new attempt to regain the power from Horthy, who three years before in Baden promised to the King with tears in his eyes that he would serve him faithfully until death.

It was quite evident that the new Hungarian regime was turning away from royalist loyalty. The anti-Habsburg behavior of the Successor States was worsening even before the Little Entente was established by the mutual assistance pacts. Benes threatened with counter-measures on March 30th and remarked that "Hungary would be in a very bad position" if the Habsburg question were not solved satisfactorily.[96] On April 2nd he said in the Czechoslovak Senate that "the Habsburg legend must end," and held out the prospect of direct intervention and the deposition of the Hungarian leaders. The Kingdom of Rumania was the only one of the Successor States which handled the problem rather discreetly, not wanting to disturb the delicate East-Central European balance of power and risk her territorial gains.

Horthy knew that after centuries of Habsburg rule the supporters of the King were deeply entrenched in key positions. He also had to realize that Benes meant what he said, and Hungary was not prepared militarily for an attack. The lasting occupation of the country, "the overturning of the Constitution, the removal of the government and the unforeseen results of a social upheaval" would have endangered the nation as well as the newly established regime."[97] If a later characterization was true and Horthy "did not understand anything of internal or external policies,"[98] he certainly had associates who were aware of the possibility of another return attempt, but apparently no precautionary measures were taken; mainly diplomatic channels were used.

The legal basis of Charles' claim was rather cloudy. The opponents of the Habsburgs frequently referred to the 7th paragraph of the Compromise law of 1867 which clearly stated that "the crown of Hungary belongs to the ruler who also rules the other countries" of the Austro-Hungarian Empire. The Pragmatic Sanction (the first three laws of 1723) also stipulated that the Hungarian throne can be occupied by a female member of the House of Habsburg, who should possess the Austrian provinces together with Hungary. According to this the ancient right of the Hungarian nation for free election of their king came to life again when the Monarchy dissolved and co-possession became impossible.

As a July 12th, 1921 telegram of Minister of Foreign Affairs Bánffy proves, the Swiss government at that time hesitated to prolong the residence permit of Charles beyond August, remembering his unathorized trip to Hungary, which resulted in Allied rebukes. This was the goal of the Little Entente states, too, because they wanted Charles to be transferred to a more distant country. As the Hungarian chargé d'affaires reported to Bánffy on July 21st, Spain was considering giving asylum to the King and his family, but no decision was expected before October. In May the Swiss Federal Council stipulated that Charles had to stay away from any kind of political activity, report his travel plans three days in advance to the Political Department, and wait for permission before leaving Hertenstein Castle, the royal family's new residence. Such humiliating rules and the uncertainty in regard to the future must have contributed to the King's decision to make a second trip to Hungary. Queen Zita's insistance was another driving factor. Charles himself was not a decision-maker, and he mostly listened to the opinion of others before doing anything important.

Hóry, the Hungarian chargé d'affaires, reported from Bucharest to the Foreign Minister on June 2nd that Rumanian government circles were convinced that King Charles intended to visit Hungary again around June 20th. He learned that the Rumanian General Staff received instructions to prepare a defensive type Czech-Rumanian military alliance; one day later the mutual assistance pact was signed. The rumors about a new restoration attempt must have contributed to the urgency.

On June 6th Bánffy instructed the chargé d'affaires in Bern to inform the Swiss Department of Foreign Affairs confidentially about the expected trip of the King. Three months later on September 2nd, chargé d'affaires Parcher reported to him that the French, British and Italian embassies asked the Federal Government of Switzerland whether it had any proof in connection with the travel plans of the former monarch. The Hungarian political police forewarned the authorities in Budapest about the King's expected return in July. Charles intended to return by boat on the Danube river in early August, but the trip was cancelled because of the visit of the Spanish Queen Mother.

Such rumors compelled Benes to turn to the President of the Peace Conference on Aug. 12th. He stated that "every Czecho-Slovak entertains feeling of profound hostility toward everything which recalls the Habsburg Monarchy and Dynasty," and added that the accession of Joseph Habsburg produced "in entire Bohemia" a feeling of astonishment, surprise and fright. It was a more precise statement than the first one, because in Slovakia a large segment of the population was pro-Habsburg and anti-Czech. That was the main reason of the tirades, and Charles must have known it. He planned a trip again in September, but his advisers asked him to postpone it because Hungary's application for membership in the League of Nations was under consideration. Rumanian Foreign Minister Take Jonescu clarified again the views of his government in an interview that was published in the August 11 issue of the Hungarian emigrant newspaper *Bécsi Magyar Hiradó*. Jonescu declared that Rumania "wouldn't tolerate a restoration. The Peace Treaty doesn't say anything about the Habsburgs. This is a fact. On the other hand, we signed the Treaty after both Austria and Hungary evicted them." Perhaps to tickle the ambition of Regent Horthy, he added: "If I would be a chauvinist Hungarian, I wouldn't consider the Habsburgs and would look for a Hungarian King..." Royalist Rumania did not pledge itself irrevocably to the other Successor States at that time and the Bucharest government apparently kept in mind the possibility of a conservative alliance consisting of Rumania, Yugoslavia and Hungary.

A police report indicated that "French royalist circles supported the return of the King and they were assisted by the Little Entente States, particularly Czechoslovakia, which hoped that the division [of Hungarian territory] might come closer if he could be tricked into this."[99] In September the news leaked out that the King wanted to leave by plane; therefore, Swiss airport authorities were instructed to demand identification from each passenger.

On October 21st, Prime Minister Bethlen made a speech in Pécs and analyzed the constitutional and legal aspects of the question. In his opinion, the 1920 law that declared the suspension of the exercise of the King's rights, and the Trianon peace treaty which recognized Hungarian independence, did not contradict the theory of legitimate succession — or the idea that Hungarians had the right to elect another King. Bethlen emphasized that "the nation through its representative government should clarify the situation with the King." It seemed that the door was finally open for Charles' return, although Bethlen added to his cunning statement that he would not accept either a "putsch" or a dethronization under any circumstances. The government wanted to negotiate and "make a decision later."

Queen Zita didn't want to wait and constantly urged her husband to do something, repeating that the first attempt ended in failure only because she was not with him. The takeover in Hungary was the slogan in the castle, but confidants of the royal couple and the servants frequently heard Zita saying that the Court would be in Schönbrunn again before Christmas. She never believed Horthy and relied on Baron Boroviczény, the King's private secretary, who worked out the details of the new trip with Archduke Maximilian.

Mrs. Boroviczény's duty was the transportation of the luggage, and Werkman, whose role in connection with the first return attempt was mentioned earlier, played the role of publicity director.[100] Swiss, Austrian and German newspapers frequently published articles about Charles, his right to the Hungarian throne, the endless negotiations with Spain and the miserable life of the royal family in Hertenstein.

Secretary Schönte was the liaison officer between the Court and the Swiss authorities. Bishop Seidel maintained connections with Rome; the Pope was informed about the King's plan.

On October 4th Schönte reported to the police that an attempt was made to murder Charles. As a result, on the 6th a detective and four guards with dogs were sent to Hertenstein for the proctection of the royal family. On the 10th, Boroviczény and his wife left the villa with heavy luggage, and told the guards that Spain was the destination of their journey, but they went to Hungary.

Around the same time, a courier of Major Ostenburg, a former Horthy supporter, arrived in Hertenstein and informed the King, that time was right for his return, because Count Gyula Andrássy, the last Foreign Minister of the Monarchy, Gusztáv Gratz, Horthy's Foreign Minister, and two other influential politicians, National Assembly Speaker István Rakovszky and Ödön Beniczky, were willing to form a government. Ostenburg advised the King to take over in Hungary at once. As it turned out later, Count Sigray, the Commissioner of Western Hungary, and Colonel Lehár, the brother of the noted composer, also supported the King.

The Austrian Socialist government guarded the Hungarian border very effectively. Hungarian guerillas operated in the Burgenland area,[101] and the asylum given in Austria to communist and other anti-Horthy emigrants also cooled the relations between the two neighbouring countries. It was therefore decided that Charles and Zita had to fly to Hungary.

On October 18th, Zita made a trip to Zürich. The King followed her on the 20th, which was the wedding anniversary of the couple. Charles' personal luggage was smuggled out through a back door of the castle and taken — partly by boat — to Luzern. Employees of the royal household, who stayed in Hertenstein, organized a banquet and drank all the champagne. Werkman granted himself a 50,000 franc sum for dismissal. The servants departed after the party, with the exception of those who took care of the children. Zita burned all bridges behind the King. She knew that there was no way back to Hertenstein castle. The adventure had to be successful, or — come what may. As it turned out, the trip was almost as troublesome as the travel of another Habsburg, the bride of Ferdinand III, who left Madrid in spring, 1630 and arrived in Vienna on February 21, 1631 for her wedding. For Charles and Zita it took considerably less than a year to complete the journey to Hungary, but quite a few surprises were waiting for them after their arrival.

There were no problems at the nearby Dübendorf airport. The royal couple was not recognized; identification papers were not required. The 180 hp. Dutch-made Junker plane, which was purchased by Boroviczéni, took off a few minutes after noon and flew at 3,500 meters with a speed of 170 km/h. Over Kampen in Bavaria, a critical situation developed because the motor stopped, and the airplane fell more than 1000 meters. Shortly after this, it started again, and at 4:10 p.m. the Junkers landed in Hungary on a farmland near the castle of Count Cziráky. There was a christening party in the castle; the royal couple did not have to starve.

Colonel Lehár and Major Ostenburg were quickly notified about the safe arrival of the King and the Queen. They were taken to the military barracks in Sopron, where a group of Hungarian aristocrats and politicians including Andrássy, Sigray, Rakovszky and Gratz — was already waiting. This time the soldiers and the officers of the local garrison had to first swear allegiance. Queen Zita wanted to be sure that beside the politicians the armed forces also supported her husband. Another oath to Horthy was taken one year before, but this did not disturb Ostenburg and Lehár. Everybody shouted loudly: "Through fire and water, on the seas, land and in the air, for God, King and Country!"

Shortly after the ceremony, the government was formed. István Rakovszky became Prime Minister; Count Gyula Andrássy Foreign Minister; Colonel Lehár received the Defense portfolio, Ödön Beniczky the Ministry of the Interior, and Gusztáv Gratz the Ministry of Finance and Commerce. The Minister of Agriculture position was not filled;

94

the Ministry of Religious Affairs and Education was offered to Count Albert Apponyi, who waited in another town.

Horthy had to thereby face the first serious challenge to his rule. A counter-government was established; it was supported by important political leaders and officers, and the partly German-Austrian population of Sopron was enthusiastic. It was an ominous sign not only for the Horthy regime, but also for the leaders of Czechoslovakia, Austria and other states which inherited national and linguistic minorities as well as the institutions and the civil service from the Habsburg Empire. The Catholic clergy had pro-Habsburg sympathies everywhere.

As Count Andrássy told a reporter of the *Manchester Guardian*, from the border city of Sopron to Győr — which is located about half way between the Austrian border and Budapest — there was no opposition. At every railroad station, troops were sworn in, pretty girls presented flowers to Zita, and the local population greeted the royal couple with "long live the King and the Queen." Admiral Horthy's first telegram reached the King in Győr. It warned him not to continue the trip. No one believed that the telegram meant military measures and the King's party continued the journey toward Budapest. Two troop-carrying trains ran at the front and two behind Charles' train.

Saturday night the King and the Queen heard cannon fire at the railroad station of Torbágy which was only 18 miles from the capitol city. Ostenburg, who had just received a promotion to General from Charles got information that the railroad was open and rushed ahead with his troops, leaving the King behind. At midnight, Ostenburg returned to Torbágy and reported to Charles that his troops had encountered machine gun fire at Budaőrs at the outskirts of Budapest. General Hegedüs also visited the King and told him that the Budapest government had asked for an armistice. The peace-loving King answered without hesitation: "Let's not attack. I didn't come to fight against my own people."

When Ostenburg asked Charles next morning whether the

fighting must go on, he replied with an emphatic "no." Shortly after that, he dismissed his officers because he was worried about their lives. The King was convinced that nobody would lay hands on the crowned ruler, and he was not afraid of Horthy's army.

Andrássy's dramatic interview was evidently one-sided, because he was not in a position to look behind the scenes. The Bethlen government learned about the King's return almost as soon as his plane landed, as was proved by a telephone conversation between Foreign Minister Bánffy and the Sopron telephone center. Next morning the official Hungarian news agency issued a short government communiqué about the King's arrival in Sopron and stated that in view of the Budapest regime, Charles could not exercise the rights of the sovereign at that time, should leave Hungarian territory again, and assured the nation and the world that the necessary measures were taken by the authorities.

Prime Minister Bethlen and Defense Minister Belitska issued an order to the commandants of the military districts asking them to stop the King and his troops, prevent the spread of the rebellion toward the East, explain the real situation to the military personnel, and withdraw east of Szombathely those troops which were stationed near the Austrian boundary line. In Bethlen's opinion "the King could not exercise the rights of a sovereign according to our laws. It is the standpoint of the government that it holds the power in the name of the Regent." Authorities and the troops were forbidden to take an oath to the King or follow his orders: "they had to obey the Regent and follow the orders of the [Budapest] government alone." Horthy issued a similar order on that day.

Rakovszky, the King's Prime Minister, telephoned Bethlen from Ács when he heard that the railroad tracks were broken up at a tunnel by government troops, and threatened with attack. Bethlen explained to Rakovszky that Minister Vass was on his way to the King's headquarters with a letter from the Regent and also carried the protesting note of the

Allies. He asked the King to wait. Rakovszky was not interested and put down the receiver.

Next day another telephone conversation took place between the two Prime Ministers. Rakovszky called Bethlen again, told him that Horthy's troops were beaten and that a cease fire order should be given to the government units. He also said that Bethlen would be responsible for the consequences, if such an order would not be given at once. According to an October 26th report of the Hungarian news agency, five minutes after the conversation "the retreat of the mutinous troops began."

The Regent's letter was delivered to Rakovszky, but it did not reach the King, whose hesitant personality was well known among his followers. Horthy referred in it to a "difficult inner struggle" and reported to the King that if he were to occupy Budapest with military force, Hungary would cease to exist forever, because of the international situation.

The government troops who opposed Ostenburg's soldiers were a mixture of regulars and anti-Habsburg college fraternity groups who were organized swiftly by Captain Gömbös and sent to the front by streetcars.[102] The royal troops fought with varying success and captured several officers and students, many of whom were maltreated. A captured colonel was forbidden to look out from the window of the King's train and was threatened with execution. Many captured students were killed by rifle butts as well as by stabbing and shooting. Major Toókos and those students who were kept alive were taken to the Budaörs railroad station and exposed to the cannon fire of the government troops for almost an hour. This was one of the reasons for the enormously large losses of the university battalions. Finally at noon additional troops arrived from the countryside and secured the victory for Horthy.

The armistice stipulations were severe and included unconditional surrender. Amnesty was promised to those who capitulated immediately, "with the exception of the instigators and leaders." The Bethlen government guaranteed the personal security of the royal couple and promised that an agreement would be made with the Allies in regard to their permanent residence. The 3rd point of the armistice agreement stated that "His Majesty should resign the Hungarian throne voluntarily and in writing."

Admiral Horthy joyously thanked the National Army and the people of Budapest in his October 24th proclamation, accusing "unknown people" who misled the King, although they must have known that the final result of his return was "foreign occupation and the annihilation of the country."

Horthy certainly had a point in connection with the danger of foreign intervention. The Czechs closed their southern border on Oct. 23rd, and on the 24th general mobilization was announced. Two days later the semi-official Avala news agency published a communiqué in Belgrade about a Czech South-Slav and Rumanian ultimatum in which the handing over of King Charles, full payment for the mobilization expenses, and complete Hungarian disarmament was demanded. The ultimatum was not delivered as the result of the intervention of the Great Powers, who wanted to preserve peace in East-Central Europe and take care of the matter alone. On October 26th, the Ambassadorial Conference of the four powers reminded the Hungarian government of earlier warnings of the Allied and Associated Powers, asked for an immediate proclamation of the dethronization of the "ex-King," and the proper guarding of Charles, who had to leave Hungarian territory. The Great Powers declared that in the case of a negative answer they would not be in a position to take the responsibility "for the acts of the neighbouring states and the result of their intervention."

Even before the threats, Bethlen must have realized that Charles' return would not have solved the country's ills. Industrial unemployment was very high. Financial resources were consumed in the war, and the remainder was smuggled abroad during the revolutionary era. The national capital dwindled to about five per cent of the estimated $180—

200,000,000 of 1910. The crown, which was the monetary unit, still linked the country with Austria, and an unprecedented inflation especially impoverished salaried employees. Unfortunately, Horthy took over many of the Monarchy's institutions, which appeared as a liability. His regime was the only one among those established on the ruins of the Habsburg Empire which did not confiscate the property of the ruling family, tolerated aristocratic privileges, and paid pension to employees of the Dual Monarchy if they resided in Hungary.[103] Horthy's traditionalist outlook encouraged Charles and the members of his entourage; therefore, he had to bear part of the responsibility for the return attempts. Double-dealing characterized the Regent's behavior in 1921. At the beginning of his rule, Horthy was vacillating between loyalty and resistance, but the uncompromising attitude of the Allies and the January 1920 elections convinced him that Charles was unwanted. Moreover, the sweet taste of power must have contributed to the change of his behavior.

On October 26th Charles and Zita were taken to the Tihany Abbey, located on an isolated peninsula in Lake Balaton.[104] Ambassador Kálmán Kánya and Count Imre Csáky accompanied them and tried to convince Charles about the necessity of his resignation. The King, for perhaps the first time in his life, was stubborn and refused to sign the resignation document. On October 28th the Ambassadorial Conference notified the Hungarian Foreign Minister in a note that the Allies were satisfied with the energetic and decisive actions which brought about the failure of the second restoration attempt. According to the note, Charles and Zita had to be taken to Budapest and escorted to the Commander of the British Danube flotilla, who would be responsible for the personal safety of the King until the Allied and Associated Powers would assign a place for his permanent residency. The Council reminded the Hungarian government that the dethronization had to be announced soon.

British Ambassador T. B. Hohler informed Foreign Minister Bánffy on October 29th that his government advised Prague not to send an ultimatum to Budapest, because the problem could be solved in a friendly way. In the opinion of the British government, the Czechoslovakian demand for the reimbursement of the mobilization cost was conflicting with the Trianon peace treaty.

The British warning was disregarded by the Prague government. Benes demanded in a quasi-ultimatum the dethronization of Charles as well as the exclusion from the throne of every member of the House of Habsburg.

His efforts were not in vain. One day later the Ambassadorial Council also stated that the resignation of Charles alone would not be acceptable, and Hungary should extend the dethronization to the entire Habsburg family.

Finally, On November 5th the National Assembly enacted the dethronization law. It declared that the Habsburgs forfeited their right to the throne and abolished the 1723 Pragmatic Sanction which secured the Hungarian throne for Habsburg descendants of both sexes and united the country "indivisibly and inseparably" with other Habsburg dominions. The Hungarian government solemnly promised that if the election of a King were to be considered, it would inform the Great Powers and would not make any decision without their consent.

The report of the Committee of Public Laws, headed by István Koszó, made it clear on November 3 that both the royal power and the co-possession of Hungary with other Kingdoms and countries represented in the former Austrian Imperial Council ceased to exist. "The National Assembly reserved for itself the drawing of the consequences for the period following the peace treaty. The exercise of the royal power, the questions of succession and the person of the King belong to those categories which the National Assembly reserved for itself. The Committee on Public Laws declares that the submission and discussion of the law was made timely by the fact according to which certain factors wanted to draw the conclusions reserved for the National Assembly one-sidedly, without asking the opinion of the National Assembly. As a result of this, serious internal and diplomatic complications were created which made neccessary the urgent legal solution of these pending questions."

The overwhelming majority of the members of the National Assembly agreed with the reasoning of the writers of the report and followed their convictions and conscience in voting for the law. The circumstances only created the opportunity for a quick decision.[105]

Charles was taken to Madeira Island, where the last ruler of the Habsburg Empire contracted flu and died in 1922. Crown prince Otto was 10 years old then, too young for the throne even in normal times, and at any rate the legitimists became a declining force in Hungarian politics.

Regent Horthy was grateful to those who suported him during the crisis. Bethlen became the undisputed possessor of executive power in the next ten years. Kánya was in charge of Hungarian foreign affairs for more than a decade. The military leaders who took sides with Horthy also served him in high positions. Colonel Rőder, who had taken steps for the capture of Charles, was promoted and became Minister of Defense in 1936. Captain Gömbös, the organizer of the resistance at Budakeszi, was Prime Minister from 1932 to 1936.

The King's unsuccessful attempts to recover his throne enabled the Horthy regime to eliminate its strongest opposition. The left had been beaten earlier, and Bethlen completed the liquidation of the right-wing extremists. Hungary was admitted to the League of Nations in 1923; the new Hungarian governmental system became seemingly acceptable to the rest of Europe, and it was the old continent which played a dominant part in international affairs between the two World Wars.

X. THE ERA OF CONSOLIDATION BEGINS

Count István Bethlen, whose administration left its mark on the next ten years of Hungarian history, became Prime Minister on April 14th, 1921. As it was mentioned earlier, before and during the war years, the Transylvanian aristocrat was a supporter of Count István Tisza's National Labor Party. During the rule of the Soviets, Bethlen emigrated to Vienna and helped to organize the Anti-Bolhevist Committee. In 1919 he initiated the organization of the Christian National Unity Party but did not join it.

Political conservatism, a peculiar kind of liberal economic views and aversion to every kind of extremist ideology characterized Bethlen. In contrast to his predecessors, he was not obligated to the royalists, and Horthy gave him a free hand in the formation of the policies of his cabinet after Count Pál Teleki resigned as the result of the first return attempt of King Charles.

In the field of foreign policy the possibilities were rather limited. The sudden changes in and around Hungary left many people in a state of shock. They sometimes felt like a man who spent several years in a lunatic asylum and was released after the war, according to a contemporary story. A passer-by explained to him in Budapest, that Austria ceased to be an Empire in 1918 and became a Republic.

'And what happened to Hungary?' asked the former patient.

'It has become an independent kingdom.'

'And who is the king?'

'Nobody. The country is ruled by Regent Horthy, a former Admiral.'

'Then Hungary still has the Adriatic seaports?'

'No. The Regent is an Admiral with no fleet,' said the stranger.

'And who got the seaports?'

'Yugoslavia, a newly organized Kingdom of the Serbs, Croats and Slovenes.'

'Then I presume that Francis Joseph still rules the Bohemians and Moravians, who were always among the most loyal subjects of the House of Habsburg.'

'No, they formed an independent Republic also, incorporating Slovakia,' answered the passer-by. 'Rumania has gotten Transylvania, another former Hungarian territory.'

'I give up,' said the man. 'They told me in the asylum that I was cured, but now I feel that I have to return there again.'

If Bethlen had any ideological basis at all, it was the revision of the Trianon peace treaty, but even that did not influence his decisions too much. His immediate goals were the pacification of the workers, formal alliance with the farmers, foreign loan and membership in the League of Nations.

Bethlen's succession to the premiership was probably the result of the General Order that Regent Horthy issued to the National Army on March 30th. Teleki objected to the Order because he did not countersign it and because it was printed in the press, although publication was prohibited by the Prime Minister's office. Bethlen did not have loyalty problems; he stood at Horthy's side during the first "putsch" attempt, and it was rather natural that the Regent asked him to form a new cabinet.

The Prime Minister's task was very difficult. Two revolutions, the counter-revolution, enemy occupation and the loss of two thirds of the land of historical Hungary created general distrust in politics. The return attempts of Charles shook up the traditional leadership; there was more disagreement than consent about the future course that Hungary had to follow.

Parliamentary life in Hungary during the era of the Dual Monarchy was restricted to obstruction and arguments in the field of national defense, finance and foreign policy, since such problems were decided upon in Vienna. The tone of the discussions at the meetings of the National Assembly continued to be rough. Political opponents frequently did not admit defeat and accused the winner of subversive agitation or other illegal actions.

The March 17, 1920 report of the Committee for Parliamentary Immunity quoted from the record of evidence of the gendarmerie which stated that Mihály Kerekes, member of the Parliament, made a speech in Sajóvámos and indicated that "the war was started by the rich and powerful. At the war fronts, poor people were sent to the trenches, but the wealthy were hiding in the hinterland. A short time ago if a rich man and a poor man had a court case, always the rich won. An influential person was simply taken to a sanitarium after embezzling a million, but the poor man was arrested if he killed a rabbit on the farm of a rich landowner." Such cases were rather common. Dénes Patacsi, Károly Hencz, János Szabó, Baron Szterényi, and others were subpoened in short succession by the Committee.[100]

The anti-communist policy of the government was documented in various ways. In July 1920 the trial of communist commissars opened in Budapest, after thorough preparation and a propaganda campaign. At about the same time Béla Kun left Austria suspecting that the Hungarian government might want to request his extradition after the first incriminating testimonies. German border authorities held him in custody and wanted to return him to Austria, but the Vienna government was unwilling to take him. Finally he was allowed to pass through to Russia on July 30th, in spite of intervention by the U. S. State Department demanding that the Austrian government hold Hungarian communist refugees until all Americans held prisoner in Russia were freed.

In August a bill was introduced in the National Assembly to authorize the use of the Hungarian army outside of frontiers to resist Bolshevist advance. At that time Horthy seriously considered a military alliance with Poland.

Earlier in May a British labor delegation had arrived in Budapest to investigate charges that Hungarian workers were mishandled and tortured by the authorities. In June the German Federation of Labor declared a boycott against Hungary because of alleged atrocities. As it used to happen, time set the mind of socialist leaders at ease, especially in Germany where post-war political, social and economic problems occupied them at home. Horthy and his Prime Ministers also could turn their attention to domestic issues. Their job was not easy.

Rising prices and the constant depreciation of currency created a favorable climate for speculative transactions. Soldiers of fortune as well as small segments of the former middle class and high society who salvaged part of their wealth, rushed to the stock market day after day. The exploiters of the state and the soldiers during the war years emerged again, and formed a parasite "new society" on the ruins of the old one. The decent majority of the population watched their activities with disgust. Meanwhile the misery of the masses was increased by the dismissal of a large number of government employees.

After the death of the King, diplomatic activities were reduced to a minimum. Hungary was still surrounded by the iron ring of the Successor States, but they were also occupied by the work of economic and political reconstruction and did not pay much attention to their conservative neighbour. An introvert, isolationist mentality characterized the dismembered country; hedonism was the only meaning of life for many of those who survived the mass slaughter of the war and the political degradation of the post-war years.

Hungarian agriculture did not lose as much as other segments of the national economy did; therefore, the government did not worry about it. The budget recommendation for the period February-April 1920 contained only 20,610 crowns for the Smallholders' Ministry, although the next smallest amount (Ministry of National Minorities) was 1,500,000 crowns and the Ministry of Commerce received 536,461,800 crowns. In addition to this, the agricultural administration was frequently attacked. Gyula Rubinek, Minister of Agriculture, asked for the investigation of a special committee when he was accused of malpractice by Albin Lingauer, a legitimist newspaper editor and member of the National Assembly.

Bethlen probably wanted to initimidate the farmers who were openly anti-communist and demanded special privileges after the counter-revolutionary takeover. On the other hand, his regime's arch-enemies were lurking in the Social Democratic Party. One of his first goals was to put the leaders of the industrial workers in their places. The Social Democrats were anti-royalist; therefore, the election of Horthy played into Bethlen's hand. *Népszava*, the party organ offered the horny hand of the workers for conciliation in an editorial on March 2, 1920, and on December 22, 1921 when the internal situation was calmer and most people had adapted themselves to the circumstances, an agreement was concluded between the government and the Social Democratic Party. The treaty granted an amnesty, secured the same right of assembly which was granted to other political parties, returned confiscated funds to the Trade Unions, and promised secret franchise in the cities. In return for these privileges, the Socialists promised that they would abstain from propaganda attacks directed against the national aims, support the government in important matters of foreign policy, and confine the activities of the workers' organizations to the economic field. The Unions were not allowed to extend their propaganda to agricultural workers. Later, in 1924 the party leaders referred to irresistible pressure and stated that the agreement had not been considered binding to the Socialists, but it secured 25 parliamentary seats for them at the 1922 elections and also consolidated the framework and the functions of the party. It is undeniable that the real winner was Bethlen, who — instead of forcing the Marxists underground — gave them a limited freedom of action and created a more or less loyal opposition for himself.

106

According to Bethlen's first policy speech, his cabinet was formed on the basis of land reform, "real democracy," the elimination of illegal acts against the industrial workers, and the reform of political representation in Parliament. After the doubledealing behavior of the Party of Christian Unity during the two return attempts of Charles, the Prime Minister had to shift his political basis to the agrarians. On January 5, 1922, Bethlen appeared at the banquet of the Smallholders' Party and made a speech in which he assaulted the Legitimists who "started an armed attack against the nation." Emphasizing the responsibility of the royalists in the preparation of revolutions and the contraction of the country to one-third of its former size, he shouted: "I have already made a decision. Whether I shall have one hundred, twenty or ten followers, I wish to establish a union with the Smallholders' Party." The party leader, István Nagyatádi Szabó, who four months earlier was involved in an export swindle, shook the hand of Bethlen amid the applause of those present who believed that they became the members of the governing party. As it turned out later, Bethlen took with him his old political friends and supporters and the fusion changed the face of the formerly agrarian peasant party.

The pre-war election law was declared still valid and in force and, when the two year mandate of the National Assembly expired on February 16, the Regent's manuscript closed the session. Two weeks later, a new election decree was put in force. It again introduced open election in the countryside and restricted the secret franchise to the cities. As a result of these measures, the newly organized National Unity Party, which was originally based on the Smallholders' Party, received 140 seats out of a total of 245. The Legitimists, Socialists, Liberals and smaller splinter groups shared the rest. Bethlen had a clear majority in Parliament; political consolidation created the groundwork for the later social, economic, and financial reconstruction, which did not solve many of the problems of the country, but provided a "modus vivendi" internally as well as with the outside world.

107

NOTES

1. Károlyi, Mihály. *Egy Egész Világ Ellen.* (Against the whole world.) Budapest: Gondolat, 1965, p. 135.
2. From the literary heritage of writer and critic F. Riedl. *Minerva* (Budapest), vol. 1, 1922, p. 137.
3. *The Messages and Papers of Woodrow Wilson.* New York: The Review of Reviews Corp., 1924, vol. 1, p. 451.
4. Macartney, C. A. *October Fifteenth; a History of Modern Hungary,* 1929-1945. Edinburgh Univ. Press, 2nd ed., 1961, pt. I, p. 21.
5. Balfour, the head of the British Special Mission in Washington, made a statement at the Imperial War Council in May, 1917, in which he accused Italy of "opening her mouth rather widely; she not only got the Allies to promise her *Italia Irredenta,* but asked for parts of Dalmatia," which could not be regarded as a natural part of Italy. *74th Congress, 2nd Session, House Document* No. 502, Pt. 2, p. 24. Such statements were rather common also at the Peace Conference.
6. "Doch halte ich einen Grossangriff des Feindes an der Front der sechsten Armee für die naechste Zeit als nicht wahrscheinlich." Rubint, Desiderius. *Daten über das Verhalten der ungarischen Truppen beim Zusammenbruch.* Budapest: Kgl. ung. Kriegsarchiv, 1923, p. 114.
7. Deák, Francis. *Hungary at the Paris Peace Conference.* New York: Columbia University Press, 1942, p. 355 (Document I).
8. Lieutenant Colonel F. Nyékhegyi.
9. "Mehrere unserer Kriegsgefangenen, die leider für diese Richtung eine grosse Meinung haben, will man aufstecken und dann über die Kampffront zurück-

senden, um hier ihre schaedlichen Ideen zu verbreiten." Honvéd District Command of Pozsony, No. 2083 Order. *Hoover Institution, Hungarian Collection.*

10. Royal Hungarian Ministry of Defense, No. 4057, eln. 1, dated March 3, 1918. Top Secret Instructions to Commandants about Russian and Entente Revolutionary Propaganda and Countermeasures for its Prevention. *Hoover Institution, Hungarian Collection.*

11. Royal Hungarian Ministry of Defense, No. 7515/1 oszt. dated March 30, 1918, and No. 12380 eln. 1., 1918 (Supplement). *Hoover Institution, Hungarian Collection.*

12. Royal Hungarian Ministry of Defense, 16180 eln. 1., dated November 5, 1915. *Hoover Institution, Hungarian Collection.* The purpose of the conference was the reactivation of the Second International, which became paralyzed by the World War. Lenin and some of his followers who attended the meetings demanded secession from the International and setting the stage for revolutions in every country, but their suggestions were voted down. The conference ended with the issuance of a Manifesto for peace without annexation and indemnification.

13. Windischgraetz, Lajos. *My Adventures and Misadventures.* London: Barrie and Rockliff, 1967, pp. 51-52.

14. Answer to Mihály Károlyi's question. Minutes of parliamentary debates. *Hoover Institution, Hungarian Collection.*

15. Seymour, Charles. *The Intimate Papers of Colonel House.* Boston: Houghton-Mifflin, 1926-28, vol. 2, p. 345.

16, *The Lansing Papers,* 1914-20. Washington: U.S. Government Printing Office, 1940, pp. 662-64.

17. Károlyi, Mihály. *Egy Egész...*, pp. 319-320.

18. According to Károlyi the collapse of the monarchy

became final when Admiral Miklós Horthy, the commander-in-chief of the Austro-Hungarian Navy, transferred the entire fleet to the South Slavs upon the order of Charles "by a protocol drawn up on the 31st [of October] in which he made mention of the 'people of the formerly existing Austro-Hungarian monarchy.'" It was therefore Horthy who first declared the non-existence of the monarchy. Károlyi, Michael. *Memoirs.* New York: E.P. Dutton, 1957, p. 115. In fact the formation of the new states on the ruins of the Habsburg empire was in progress everywhere by that time.

19. Gratz, Gusztáv. *A Forradalmak Kora. Magyarország Története,* 1918-1920. (The revolutionary era. The history of Hungary, 1918-1920.) Budapest: Magyar Szemle Társaság, 1935, pp. 32-33.

20. *Az Est,* January 27, 1917.

21. Jászi, Oscar. *Revolution and counter-revolution in Hungary.* New York: H. Fertig, 1969, pp. 1-2.

22. Document found in the private archives of Count Andrássy. It was copied by Sándor Pethő, a newspaperman, who was commissioned to sort and arrange the archival collection of the Andrássy family after the war. *Hoover Institution, Hungarian Collection.*

23. Earlier, in October Andrássy requested separate peace from Washington and advised Károlyi "to appease the lunatics and hysterical Jews and wait for (President) Wilson's answer, after which the Károlyi government could take over, in three weeks time." Károlyi, M. *Egy egész...,* p. 117.

24. Szilassy, Julius. *Der Untergang der Donau Monarchie.* Berlin: Verlag Neues Vaterland, 1921, pp. 330-31. Mostly newspapermen represented Hungary abroad during the Károlyi era.

25. Böhm, Vilmos. *A Munkások és a Termelés.* (The wor-

kers and the problems of production.) Budapest: Népszava Könyvkereskedés, 1919, p. 13.

26. "The Czechs were the first to enter Hungarian territory at the end of 1918." Horthy, Nicholas. *Memoirs.* New York: Robert Spellers and Sons, 1957, p. 96.

27. Károlyi M. *Egy Egész...*, p. 133.

28. All three cities had in majority Magyar population. The injustice of the armistice line which was forced upon Károlyi was proved by the peace treaty itself in 1920. It awarded Pécs and Baja to Hungary.

29. Böhm, Wilhelm. *Im Kreuzfeuer Zweier Revolutionen.* Münich: Verlag für Kulturpolitik, 1924, p. 109. The author was Minister of Defense in the Károlyi (Berinkey) government and Commander-in-Chief of the Hungarian Red Army.

30. The United States, together with its allies, wanted to preserve the unity of Austria-Hungary, until the disintegration of the multi-national state became evident. Seymour, C. *The Intimate...*, vol. 3, p. 336. President Wilson's foreign policy was both nationalist and internationalist. This is one of the explanations of the ambiguity, "rightly attributed to the Wilsonian principles." Bárány, George. "Wilsonian Central Europe: Lansing's Contribution." *Historian,* vol. 28, 1966, p. 250.

31. Tőkés, Rudolf. *Béla Kun and the Hungarian Soviet Republic.* New York: Praeger, 1967, pp.123-125.

32. Hoover, Herbert. *Memoirs.* New York: Macmillan, 1951, vol. 1, p. 398.

33. *Századok,* vol. 100, no. 6, 1966, p. 1264.

34. *Századok,* vol. 100, no. 1, 1966, p. 110.

35. The original telegram is in the possession of the Hoover Institution. *TS, Hungary,* A2, Box,1. Hungarian emigrants were also seeking foreign help and worked against the Soviet government from the beginning.

Count Gyula Andrássy suggested Allied military intervention already on March 27th, 1919. Gratz Gusztáv, ed. *A Bolsevizmus Magyarországon.* (Bolshevism in Hungary.) Budapest Franklin Társulat, 1921, p. 109.

36. Ullman, R. H. *Britain and the Russian Civil War.* Princeton, Princeton Univ. Press, 1968, p. 139.

37. When Károlyi introduced his associates at the armistice negotiations in Belgrade, General D'Esperay remarked contemptuously: "Vout étes déja tombés si bas?" (Have you sunk so low?) Horthy, M. *Memoirs,* p. 132. Apparently he expressed official French opinion when he said that "Hungarians marched with the Germans and will be punished with them."

38. Kun's report on foreign affairs at the June 16-25 National Congress of Councils.

39. Crafford, F. S. *Jan Smuts: a Biography.* New York: Doubleday, 1943, pp. 156-157.

40. Magyar Hadügyi Népbiztosság (Commissariat of Defense). Nos. 331/151 and 332/151. *Eln. 5. Osztály. Hoover Institution, Hungary, XII.*

41. Government telegram, addressed to the Leipziger Volkszeitung, dated June 24, 1919. *Hoover Institution, TS. Hungary, A2, Box* 1.

42. Government telegram, addressed to the Leipziger Volkszeitung, dated June 24, 1919. *Hoover Institution, TS, Hungary, A2, Box* 2.

43. Kirschner, Béla. *A Szakszervezeti Kormány Hat Napja.* (Six days of the Trade Union government.) Budapest: Kossuth Könyvkiadó, 1968, p. 12.

44. *American Commission to Negotiate Peace,* Paris, 1918-1919. Cases 185.002 to 185.007. National Archives, Washington, D.C.

45. Low, Alfred D. "The Soviet Hungarian Republic and the Paris Peace Conference." *Transactions of the American Philosophical Soc.,* vol. 53, pt. 10, pp. 85-86.

46. Szinai, Miklós and Szücs László, eds. *Horthy Miklós Titkos Iratai.* (The secret documents of Miklós Horthy.) Budapest: Kossuth Könyvkiadó, 1963, p. 11.

47. Wandycz, Piotr S. *France and Her Eastern Allies.* Minneapolis: The University of Minnesota Press, 1962, p. 187. President Wilson also believed in 1917, "in common with the leading statesmen of Europe," that the political union of Austro-Hungarian peoples was a necessity, and felt that once freed from German domination, the Habsburg monarchy would prove a beneficial force. Some of his advisers thought that American policy toward that country had to consist "first in stirring up nationalist discontent and then in refusing to accept the extreme logic of this discontent which would be the dismemberment of Austria-Hungary." Seymour, C. *The Intimate . . .,* vol. 3, p. 336.

48. Typewritten copy. *Hoover Institution, Hungarian Collection.*

49. Windischgraetz, Lajos. *My Adventures . . . ,* p. 117.

50. Government telegram addressed to the Leipziger Volkszeitung, dated April 19, 1919. *Hoover Institution, TS, Hungary,* A2 Box 1.

51. Government telegram addressed to the Leipziger Volkszeitung, dated June 21, 1919. *Hoover Institution, TS, Hungary,* A2, Box 1.

52. Kirschner, B. A. *Szakszervezeti Kormány . . . ,* p. 47.

53. Kun was the actual head of the government, but held the position of the Commissar of Foreign Affairs. — He was employed by a workers' insurance organization before the war. In Russian captivity, Kun became the president of the International Federation of Communist Prisoners of War. After returning to Hungary in November 1918, he was the recognized leader of the new Communist Party. Kun emigrated to the Soviet Union from Austria in 1920, and was a member

of the Executive Committee of the Comunist International between 1921 and 1936. He was arrested and executed during the Stalinist purges.

54. Karsai, Elek. *A Budai Sándor Palotában Történt.* (It happened in the Sándor Palace in Buda.) Budapest: Táncsics Könyvkiado, 1963, pp. 8-9.
55. Deák, F. *Hungary . . .* , p. 104.
56. Sulyok, Dezső. *Magyar Tragédia.* (Hungarian tragedy). Newark, N. J.: Style Printing Co., 1954, p. 251. Macartney, C. A. *Hungary: A Short History.* Chicago: Aldine Publ. Co., 1962, p. 205. (Prof. Macartney believes that Kun fled to Vienna on August 4.)
57. Karsai, E. *A Budai Sándor Palotában . . .* , p. 10.
58. An Allied order temporarily halted the Rumanian army at the same time. *N. Y. Times* (August 3, 1919, p. 1.)
59. Karsai, E. *A Budai Sándor Palotában . . .* , p. 17.
60. In November 1919 he was sentenced to death and executed on December 29 together with 13 Lenin Boys.
61. *Hoover Institution, Hungary,* XII, Appendix, p.1.
62. Gratz, G. *A Forradalmak . . .* , p. 229.
63. *Hoover Institution, Hungary,* XII, Appendix, p. 1.
64. Hoover, H. *Memoirs,* Vol. 1, p. 400.
65. *American Commission to Negotiate Peace,* Paris, 1918-1919. Cases 181.9202 to 181.9220. National Archives, Washington, D.C.
66. *The Hungarian Question in the British Parliament.* London: Grant Richards, 1933, p. 12. The Rumanian opinion was different. "The Rumanian Commander has reported to Bucharest that the behavior of American and British Missions becomes from day to day more unbearable," as General Bandholtz informed the American Peace Commission on October 19th. The Rumanian report was probably captured by the Allied Military Mission.

67. *Hoover Institution, Hungary,* XII, Appendix, p. 1. After the coup Csillery took over the Ministry of Public Health in the Friedrich cabinet, and was in office for four months. In 1922 he became the Director of the Social Security System. In the 1930's he represented the Northern District of Budapest in the parliament, first as a member of the Christian (Catholic) Party, and later as a supporter of the majority Party of Unity.

68. The discussion of the members of the government and the events which followed the interruption of the session are described in the minutes of the Council of Ministers, dated August 6, 1919. *Hoover Institution, Hungary,* XII, Supplement 1, pp. 1-4.

69. Horthy, M. *Memoirs,* p. 102.

70. Securing the freedom of navigation and free access to the sea was one of the favored topics of the American delegation. M. O. Hudson emphasized at the peace negotiations on May 12, 1919 that "the Allies were making Hungary into an enclaved State and by doing so they incurred a heavy responsibility." *American Commission to Negotiate Peace,* Paris, 1918-1919. Cases 185.23 to 185.372. On May 14th, upon the suggestion of Lloyd George, it was agreed that "a clause should be inserted in the Treaty providing for access of Austria and Hungary to the sea, and a Committee was nominated to prepare a suitable article." The problem wasn't solved satisfactorily.

71. "A cry arose from ... Eastern Europe to Paris, 'The Habsburgs are coming back.' " Hoover, Herbert. *The Ordeal of Woodrow Wilson.* New York: McGraw-Hill, 1958, p. 138.

72 *Budapesti Közlöny* (Official Gazette). August 9, 1919, p. 1.

73. Hoover, H. *Memoirs,* vol. 1, p. 401.

74. *American Commission to Negotiate Peace, Paris,* 1918-1919. Cases 181.9201 to 181.9202. National Archives, Washington, D. C.

75. He was a faithful subordinate of his Emperor-King. When a correspondent of a Hungarian newspaper wrote an article on the occasion of his being wounded in a naval battle at Otranto and implicated that Horthy's thoughts abandoned often the imperial headquarters and returned to the Hungarian fatherland, he said to the newspaperman: "Remember that, if my chief war lord is in Baden, then my fatherland is also there." Jászi, Oscar. *The Dissolution of the Habsburg Monarchy.* Chicago: The University of Chicago Press, 1929, p. 142.

76. Karsai, Elek and Pamlényi, Ervin: *A Fehér Terror.* (The White Terror.) Budapest: Művelt Nép, 1951, p. 28.

77. Horthy acknowledged "the frequent outbursts against Communists and Jews" in his *Memoirs* and remarked that they were "regrettable." The Allies finally sent U.S. Army Colonel Yates to Budapest in October to reorganize the police and the gendarmery.

78. Macartney, C. A. *October Fifteenth . . .* , vol. 1, pp. 28-29.

79. As he grew older, Horthy was frequently vacillating and lost his organizational abilities. In October, 1944 the Germans and their Hungarian supporters needed only one day to have him sign a document in which he abdicated from the office of Regent and another that declared the armistice proclamation of October 15 null and void. The coercion is explainable by the fact that his only surviving son's life was in danger, still the resistance that he had shown was small.

80. According to an eyewitness account, police and army officers formed a ring around the Parliament, and af-

ter 9 a.m. groups larger than three persons were dissolved. Frank, László. *Cafe Atlantis*. Budapest: Gondolat, 1963, p. 35.

81. Huszár resigned repeatedly, according to the *Documents of the National Assembly*. Authenticated edition. Budapest: Pesti Könyvnyomda Co., 1920, vol. 1. The relationship between Horthy and Huszár cooled down after the intrusion of officers to the Parliament building and the murder of two Social Democratic newspapermen on February 17th.

82. *The Messages and Papers of Woodrow Wilson*, vol. 1, p. 447.

83. 1910 Census.

84. Macartney, C. A. *Hungary ...*, p. 206.

85. See also No. 28 and 37 footnotes.

86. Molnár, Erik, ed. *Magyarország Története*. (The history of Hungary). Budapest: Gondolat, 1967, vol. 2, p. 375.

87. *IV. Károly Visszatérési Kisérletei*. (The Return Attempts of Charles IV.) Edited and published by the [Hungarian] Ministerium. Budapest: Printing office of Budapesti Hirlap. No date, pp. 69-70, Document No. 4. Upon the request of Károlyi, Dr. Török initiated negotiations with Italian Foreign Minister Sonnino in Rome in March 1915, asking Italian support of eventual Hungarian independence and separate peace. In 1916 Török lived in Switzerland and informed Károlyi about his talks with Allied and neutral diplomats and politicians.

88. Public Law I, 1920. — It spoke about "provisionary discharge of the duties of the Head of State," declaring that the King had not exercised his power since November 13, 1918; therefore, the election of a Regent was necessary.

89. Horthy said in a speech in Székesfehérvár on October 27, 1920 that "the Regent, who was elected by the National Assembly to resume supreme power for the period of the suspension of the King's rule, cannot misuse this power, cannot reach for the King's throne. I interpret my duties this way." He informed Charles periodically about the internal and external affairs of Hungary at that time.

90. Karsai, E. *A Budai Sándor Palotában* ..., p. 45.

91. Szinai, M. and Szücs, L. *Horthy Miklós* ..., pp. 18-19.

92. Horthy, M. *Memoirs,* pp. 116-117.

93. *Documents of the National Assembly.* Authenticated ed. Budapest: Pesti Könyvnyomda Co., 1920, vol. 1.

94. Windischgraetz, L. *My Adventures* ..., pp. 122-123.

95. As the years went by, Teleki became a loyal follower of the Regent. In 1939 when he was Prime Minister again, Teleki told J. F. Montgomery, the U. S. envoy to Budapest, that the re-establishment of the Dual-Monarchy would be a grave mistake and a Habsburg restoration was undesirable. S. Szilassy. "Magyar Semlegességi Törekvések 1939-ben." (Hungarian neutrality efforts in 1939.) *Új Látóhatár,* July-August 1968, p. 325-326.

96. Telegram of Tahy, the Hungarian envoy in Prague, dated March 30, 1921. *IV. Károly* ..., p. 91.

97. *Ibid,* Suppl., p. 19.

98. The December 10, 1943 report of Edmund Veesenmayer, who in 1944 became German Plenipotentiary in Hungary.

99. *IV. Károly* ..., p. 171.

100. A Hungarian police report stated that Mrs. Werkman and her sister, Miss Cantora, worked as professional spies during the war, in close cooperation with Bolgyai. Miss Cantora had good relations with the left wing of the German Social Democratic Party. When Erzberger

died, Mrs. Werkman had a requiem celebrated in the King's chapel. The Swiss police kept her under surveillance when the King and his associates lived in the Hotel National. *IV. Károly ...* , p. 172. Matthias Erzberger whose name was repeatedly mentioned in the police reports, was the leader of the left wing of the Catholic Centrum Party in Germany. As the head of the German delegation, he signed the armistice in Compiegne on November 11, 1918. In 1920, members of a rightist organization killed him.

101. In the middle of October a conference was held in Venice between Hungary and Austria, upon the intervention of Italian Foreign Minister Toretta. The disputed area was divided into two zones and plebiscite was held in Zone A. About 75 per cent of the population voted to remain in Hungary.

102. Both Bethlen and Gömbös were in Pécs when the news of the King's arrival reached them. They rushed back to Budapest.

103. Bethlen himself did not make a secret of it that serious errors were made in the field of internal politics during the years of his premiership. As he told a representative of the Smallholders' Party in 1937, "it was impossible to oppose the military dictatorship." Sulyok, Dezső. *Magyar ...* , p. 299.

104. The Tihany apartment of Charles was considered a shrine by the royalists and shown to visitors for a fee during the entire Horthy era.

105. Polónyi, Dezső. *A Magyar Királykérdés.* Budapest: Athenaeum, 1928, p. 71.

106. *Documents of the National Assembly,* 1920. Vol. 1, p. 149.

The open letter of Count Mihály Károlyi to his voters, published in the September 8, 1918 issue of the daily Magyarország.

...The first prerequisite of the peace negotiations is the democratization of the states, and the realization of the peoples' will everywhere, including our country.

The other prerequisite of the peace negotiations may be created if we can prove that we do not surrender to the concept of "Mitteleuropa." We should say openly that we want democracy and wish to be independent of everybody else, even the Germans... But our Foreign Minister and our government are silent. Only their real boss: Count István Tisza is always shouting against peace, and rattling the sword of the Germans. We should not tolerate the passiveness of our government any longer. We demand the convocation of the Parliament and the parliamentary delegations to give an opportunity to our ministers to speak and to give an account to the nation.

Let's take into our hand the thread of the peaceful settlement by declaring: we accept as a basis for negotiations the peace program of Wilson, the President of United States. This declaration wouldn't mean to accept every letter of every word of Wilson's proposal and the submission to his ideas without any negotiations. The program of the President of the United States provides the basis for a quickly arranged peace negotiation, and the creation of a peace founded on the comprehension and agreement of the people. Wilson himself surely doesn't want to push through here in Hungary the self-determination of the nationalities in its doctrinaire clarity, ignoring the historical background. This, considering our conditions, would not be more viable than the paper power which Lenin and Trotzkii would like to establish in Russia by the implementation of their state doctrine.

Time is wearing on and the matter is pressing. Let's not wait until we play out our last trump-card. We should remember the words of the poet: "The heavy stone is flying. No one knows where it will stop and whom it will hit..."

Austria-Hungary Requests Separate Peace
(Communicated through the Swedish government on
October 29, 1918)

In reply to the note of President Wilson to the Austro-
Hungarian government, dated October 18 of this year, and
the decision of the President to take up, with Austria-Hungary
separately, the question of armistice and peace, the Austro-
Hungarian government has the honor to declare that it ad-
heres both to the previous declaration of the President and
his opinion of the rights of the peoples of Austria-Hungary,
notably those of the Czecho-Slovaks and the Jugo-Slavs
contained in his last note. Austria-Hungary having thereby
accepted all the conditions which the President had put upon
entering into negotiations on the subject of armistice and
peace, nothing, in the opinion of the Austro-Hungarian government, longer stands in the way of beginning those negotiations. The Austro-Hungarian government therefore declares itself ready to enter, without waiting for the outcome
of other negotiations, into negotiations for a peace between
Austria-Hungary and the Entente States and for an immediate armistice on all the fronts of Austria-Hungary and
begs President Wilson to take the necessary measures to that
effect.

The November 13, 1918 Manifesto of King Charles IV

Ever since my accession to the throne I made efforts to deliver my people from the horrors of the war, in the outbreak of which I had no part.

I wouldn't like it if my person would be an obstacle in the free development of the Hungarian nation, which I love unalterably.

For this reason I resign of every participation in the conduct of state affairs and recognize in advance the decision in regard to Hungary's future form of state.

Dated in Eckartsau, on the thirteenth day of November, nineteen-hundred and eighteen.

The March 21, 1919 Manifesto of the Socialist Party
of Hungary and the Revolutionary Governing Council

As of today, the proletariat of Hungary takes all power in its hands.

The complete collapse of the bourgeois world and the bankruptcy of the coalition government forces the workers and peasants of Hungary to take this decisive step. The capitalistic production is in ruins; the workers are unwilling to put their heads into the yoke of the big businessmen and rich landowners.

The country can be saved from the anarchy of collapse only by the creation of socialism and communism.

At the same time, the Hungarian revolution reached the point of complete catastrophy in the field of foreign policy. The Paris Peace Conference decided to occupy militarily almost the entire territory of Hungary, considers the demarcation line a final political boundary line and by this makes the feeding [of Hungarians] and the supply of coal for revolutionary Hungary definitely impossible.

In this situation, the Hungarian revolution has only one way of saving itself; the dictatorship of the proletariat, the rule of the workers and the agrarian paupers.

The most important basis of the proletarian dictatorship is the complete unity of the proletariat. For this reason, and because of historical necessity, the Social Democratic Party of Hungary and the Communist Party of Hungary declared their union. In the future, one proletarian party, the Socialist Party of Hungary, includes every Hungarian working man and working woman.

The administrative power is being taken over by a Revolutionary Governing Council. The duty of this Council is to organize in the whole country the Councils of Workers, Peasants and Soldiers. The legislative, administrative and judiciary power is being exercised by the dictatorship of the Worker, Peasant and Soldier Councils.

Hungary is being transformed into a Republic of Councils. The Revolutionary Governing Council immediately inaugurates changes to prepare and establish socialism and communism.

The nationalization of the big farms, mines, the large factories, banks and public transportation facilities is being declared. Agrarian reform goes into effect not by land distribution, but by the organization of socialist cooperatives.

Profiteers and the sharks of food products, the exploiters of the hunger and raggedness of the masses will be prosecuted.

Iron discipline requires the execution of the counter-revolutionary bandits as well as the brigands of looting.

A huge proletarian army will be organized by which the dictatorship of the proletariat will be enforced against the Hungarian capitalists and landowners as well as the Rumanian Boyars and the Czech bourgeois.

Complete ideological and spiritual partnership is declared with the Russian Soviet government; we offer military alliance to the proletarians of Russia. Friendly greetings to the workers of England, France, Italy and America; we ask them not to tolerate for one minute the marauding campaign against the Hungarian Republic of Councils. The workers of Bohemia, Rumania, Serbia and Croatia should establish military alliance [with Hungary] against the bourgeois, the Boyars, the big landholders and the dynasties. We call on the workers of German Austria and Germany to follow the example of the Hungarian workers, bury the past, ally with Moscow, establish a Soviet Republic and oppose the conquering imperialists with weapons in their hands...

The Socialist Party of Hungary
The Revolutionary Governing Council

Declaration on the discussions between Sir George R. Clerk, Admiral Horthy and the party leaders, dated November 5, 1919

Commander-in-Chief Miklós Horthy had a conference this afternoon in the apartment of Sir George Clerk with the leaders of the National Party, the National Democratic Bourgeois Party, the Smallholders Party led by István Nagyatádi Szabó, and the Social Democratic Party. The Commander-in-Chief authorized the participants to publish his follownig statement:

The entry of the army into Budapest shall not result in military dictatorship. The army subordinates itself to the government to be established by the intervention of the Entente commissioner. The Commander-in-Chief emphasized that the army stands on the basis of equal civil rights, shall relentlessly stamp out even the germs of Bolshevism, and would not tolerate agitation on the part of the members of the army against civil rights.

Participants at the conference: Márton Lovászi, Dr. Vilmos Vázsonyi, István Nagyatádi Szabó, Ernő Garami and Lajos Varjassy.

Signed by:

      Márton Lovászi   Dr. Vilmos Vázsonyi
      Ernő Garami   Horthy

*Admiral Horthy's speech made on November 16, 1919,
when he entered Budapest at the head of his troops*

Mr. Mayor! In the name of the Hungarian National Army,
I offer you my sincere thanks for your warm words of welcome. Today, on the threshold of this city, I am not prepared
to speak in conventional phrases. My sense of justice compels
me to tell you plainly what is uppermost in my mind at this
moment. When we were still far, when our hope of returning
to this poor, ill-fated city, arms in hand, was the merest glimmer, we cursed and hated her, for from afar we saw only
the mire into which she had sunk and the persecution and
martydom which our Hungarian brethren were suffering.

The Hungarian nation has always loved and admired Budapest, this city which, in recent months, has been its degradation. Here, on the banks of the Danube, I arraign her. This
city has disowned her thousand years of tradition, she has
dragged the Holy Crown and the national colors in the dust,
she has clothed herself in red rags. The finest of the nation
she threw into dungeons or drove into exile. She laid in ruin
our property and wasted our wealth.

Yet the nearer we approached to this city, the more rapidly
did the ice in our hearts melt. We are now ready to forgive
her. We shall forgive this misguided city if she will turn
from her false gods to the service of the fatherland...

My soldiers, after they had gathered in the harvest, took
up arms to restore order in the country. Now their hands
are held out unencumbered to you in friendly greeting; but
these hands remain ready to mete out punishment and to
strike blows should the need arise. May God grant that this
need shall not arise, that the guilty, having seen the error of
their ways, may strive to play their part in rebuilding a
Budapest that shall embody the best of Hungarian virtues.

We extend to our fellow sufferers, who have endured so
much tribulation and who yet gave us their sympathy, our
heartfelt salutation.

The October 17, 1920 speech of Regent Miklós Horthy in Székesfehérvár

Recently one can observe trends which attempt to push into the foreground the question of the King's person. We all agree in it that this country, instead of denying its one thousand year old past, should continue its life as a kingdom in the great community of nations. We all would like to see the Crown of St. István sparkling in its old glory. Until we can reach this goal, complicated tasks are waiting for us in the field of foreign affairs and the difficult work of internal consolidation must also be finished.

Those who throw in the question of the King's person prematurely, disrupt the unity of the nation, revolutionize the souls of the citizens of this country, hinder the internal consolidation and by these cripple our diplomatic activities.

I know there are some who are not guided by traditions but keep such problems alive for selfish reasons or viciously wish to disrupt or stop the healing process which the nation needs after the destructive war and revolutions. There are others who work with the dirty tools of slander and suspicion for sowing distrust and disruption, not sparing my person either; sometimes well intentioned, at other times malevolently.

Everybody would have to realize that the Regent of Hungary who was elected by the National Assembly for the period of the suspension of royal power as the keeper of the supreme power, cannot abuse this power, and cannot reach for the royal power and the King's throne. In interpret my duties this way. Others should also understand what their duties are. Those who are unwilling to do this we will force to understand their duties. There is no time left for experimentation; if someone does not accept the legal system, he will be punished.

After the struggles of the first year I would like to start the second one under the sign of general calm which will finally enable us with God's help to reestablish a rich and powerful Hungary, led by a crowned King who will be welcomed by the nation with great enthusiasm and outstretched arms.

The telegram of Foreign Minister Gratz to chargé d'affaires Hóry to Bucharest

Budapest, April 8, 1921

I wish to inform you that the Yugoslav and Czechoslovak commissioners received instructions from their governments to deliver an ultimatum demanding the departure of King Charles before Thursday. The instructions were not executed because King Charles left the country in the meantime.

Gratz

The Czechoslovakian-Rumanian Treaty

The Rumanian and Czechoslovakian governments agreed in the following text of the defense agreement established between the Czechoslovak Republic and the Kingdom of Rumania:

Firmly resolving to maintain the peace which was obtained by grave sacrifices and which will be included in the planned League of Nations pact on one hand, and the situation originating in the treaty signed between the Allied and Associated Powers and Hungary on June 4, 1921 on the other hand, the President of the Czechoslovak Republic and His Majesty the King of Rumania agreed to establish a defensive agreement. For this purpose the President of the Czechoslovak Republic appointed Ferdinand Veverka, the Envoy and Minister Plenipotentiary of the Czechoslovak Republic in Bucharest, and His Majesty the King of Rumania appointed Foreign Minister Take Jonescu who after the mutual presentation of their credentials and their acceptance as faultless agreed in the following paragraphs:

1st paragraph. If Hungary, without provocation, would attempt an attack against any of the high signatory parties, the other party undertakes the obligation to rush to the defense of the attacked party using measures which are listed in the 2nd paragraph of this agreement.

2nd paragraph. The officials of the Czechoslovak Republic and the Kingdom of Rumania shall define in a military agreement to be established later the measures which are absolutely necessary for the execution of this present agreement.

3rd paragraph. Neither of the high signatory parties can establish a treaty of alliance with a third power without the notification of the other party.

4th paragraph. The two governments, in order to coordinate their peace efforts, accept an obligation to establish an agreement to bring under control their foreign policies in regard to their relationship to Hungary.

5th paragraph. This agreement will be in effect for two years from the day of the exchange of the ratification documents. After this period, any of the signatory parties may terminate this agreement, but it will remain in effect for six months after termination.

6th paragraph. The League of Nations will be notified about this agreement. (League of Nations Charter Part 7.)

7th paragraph. To certify this agreement, the plenipotentiaries signed it and affixed their seal on it.

Written in two copies in Bucharest, the 23rd day of April, 1921.

Ferdinand Veverka
Take Jonescu

The Dethronization Law of 1921

Public Law XLVII About the Termination of the Royal Rights of His Majesty Charles IV and the Succession of the House of Habsburg to the Throne.

1st Paragraph. The royal rights of Charles IV ceased to exist.

2nd Paragraph. The Pragmatic Sanction which was included in Public Laws I and II of 1723 and all of the other legal rules which defined and stated the right of the Austrian House (Domus Austriaca) to succession to the Hungarian throne became void and by this the right of the election of a king returned to the nation.

3rd Paragraph. The nation maintains the traditional form of state of kingdom without any change, but the throne will not be filled until a later period of time and the *ministerium* is instructed to make recommendations in connection with this at an appropriate time.

4th Paragraph. This law becomes effective on the day of its promulgation.

137

Mackensen, August von, General, 29
Magasházy, Major, 85
Magyarization, 12, 13
Makó, battle of, 37
Masaryk, Tomas Garrigue, 18
Marie, Queen of Rumania, wife of Ferdinand I, 81
Maximilian Habsburg, Archduke, 92
May 1 mass meeting, 39
Merging of the Social Democratic and Communist parties,
    32-33, 38
Meskó, Zoltán, 88
Miákits, Ferenc, 70
Miles, Sherman, Colonel, 30
Mongolian invasion 11
Munro, Dr., British Food Commission member, 57

Nagyatádi Szabó, István, 53, 67
— supports Bethlen, 107
National Committee of Rumanian Unity, 18
National Council, Hungarian, 20-21, 22, 23
National Army, 65
— enters Budapest, 69
National Assembly elected, 70
National Assembly of Councils, 38
Nationalities, 11-14
Nationalization, 38

Open election, 107
Ostenburg, Gyula, Major, 94, 95, 97
Ottó, Crown Prince, son of Charles I, 81

Padua, armistice of, 9
Pallavicini, Count György, 57
Paris Peace Conference, 30, 36, 41, 42, 48, 64, 82
— invites Hungarian representatives, 70
Pasic, Nikola, Serbian Prime Minister, 15
Pattantyus Ábrahám, Dezső, 63, 65
Peidl, Gyula, 9, 49, 50, 52, 56, 60, 61, 62, 63
— appointed Prime Minister, 49
— personality, 49
Penfield, Frederic C., American diplomat, 17
People's Republic, 24, 63
Peyer, Károly, 43, 50, 61, 70
Pogány, József, 33, 39

138

Ultimatum sent to Serbia, 7
Ultimatum to Hungary planned, 98
Unemployment, 98
U.S. intervention for the detention of Communist in
    Austria, 104
Urbanization, 13

Vasilescu, General, 56
Vázsonyi, Vilmos, 67, 126
Vaux, de, 26
Vienna Royal Chamber, 11
Vörös Ujság (Red News), 31
Vyx note, 31, 32, 33, 35

Wage increases, 38
War losses, 5
Wekerle, Sándor, 17, 52
Weltner, Jenő, 38, 44
Werbőczy. István, 81
Werkman, Captain, 79, 92, 93
White House Organization, 61
Wilhelm II, Emperor of Germany, 16, 26
Wilson, Woodrow, President, 1, 8 18, 19, 29, 35, 73
    — Fourteen Points 8, 20, 122
    — message to Congress, 6-7
Windischgraetz, Prince Lajos, 16, 19, 42, 83
Workers' Council, 33, 46

Yates, Colonel. 116

Zimmerwald, conference of, 11
Zita, Queen, wife of Charles I, 80, 92, 93, 94, 99

APPENDIX

TABLE OF CONTENTS

Page

Cb